"Dr Ratcliffe compassionately explores how and why emotionally driv‹
over time and, importantly, provides a step-by-step roadmap for chan
now. Underpinned by years of experience in weight management, and bro
book is an essential read for anyone wanting to break free from emotiona
— **Dr Sarah Appleton**, Highly ‹
Healthy Weight Programn

‿yıSt,
‿ıomas' Hospital

"Dr Ratcliffe has done it again, an invaluable companion on a difficult journey, this time navigating the complex issue of emotional eating – this will become another go-to resource for many people."
— **Ken Clare,** Director of Operations Obesity UK

UNDERSTANDING AND MANAGING EMOTIONAL EATING

This highly accessible therapy workbook is designed to help individuals who are engaged in weight management and obesity treatments improve their relationship with food and manage their emotional eating.

Emotional eating is a very common and distressing problem for many people who are trying to manage their weight. Emotional eating can contribute to weight gain and/or difficulties losing weight. It can also have a psychological impact, as people often feel very ashamed, frustrated and self-critical about their difficulties in stopping this behaviour. Instead of trying to address these emotional eating patterns through dieting or focusing on food, the approach presented in this workbook focuses on understanding the psychological and emotional drivers for the behaviour. Drawing on ideas from Cognitive-Behavioural Therapy, Compassion-focused Therapy and Acceptance and Commitment Therapy, the book is a step-by-step programme to help you develop a detailed understanding of the psychological drivers for your emotional eating behaviour and will help you develop a range of psychological strategies to manage your emotions and thoughts about food. The workbook contains practical resources and exercises, and by the end of the programme, you will have developed your own Emotional Eating Manual.

This therapy workbook is for people who are unhappy with their emotional eating habits and the impact these have on their emotional health. It is also a valuable resource for therapists, dietitians and other allied professionals who work with this population.

Dr Denise Ratcliffe is a Consultant Clinical Psychologist who has specialised in providing psychological therapy for people with emotional eating patterns and weight difficulties since 2007. She is the author of *Living With Bariatric Surgery: Managing Your Mind and Your Weight*. She worked in the NHS for 20 years and now works in private practice.

UNDERSTANDING AND MANAGING EMOTIONAL EATING

A Psychological Skills Workbook

Denise Ratcliffe

Routledge
Taylor & Francis Group

LONDON AND NEW YORK

Designed cover image: ©Getty

First published 2025
by Routledge
4 Park Square, Milton Park, Abingdon, Oxon, OX14 4RN

and by Routledge
605 Third Avenue, New York, NY 10158

Routledge is an imprint of the Taylor & Francis Group, an informa business

© 2025 **Denise Ratcliffe**

British Library Cataloguing-in-Publication Data
A catalogue record for this book is available from the British Library

ISBN: **9781032664361** (hbk)
ISBN: **9781032664347** (pbk)
ISBN: **9781032664354** (ebk)

DOI: 10.4324/9781032664354

Typeset in Interstate
by Apex CoVantage, LLC

CONTENTS

FIGURES

ACKNOWLEDGEMENTS

I would like to thank the many patients who have been generous and courageous in sharing their experiences of emotional eating and the impact that this has had on them over the years. Their generosity has allowed me to develop and refine my psychological skills and approach. I hope that this book is a source of support and hope for those who currently feel trapped by their emotional eating patterns.

I would like to extend my grateful thanks to the talented and committed group of psychologists who have guided my thinking and helped me bring this project to fruition – in particular, Dr Esme Banting, Dr Sarah Appleton, Dr Hannah Jerome, Dr Jo Ashcroft, Dr Danny O'Toole and Anne-Marie Lewis.

As always, thank you to my parents, sister and brother-in-law who have provided endless support and encouragement. I am incredibly lucky and fortunate to have you. A special acknowledgement to Alan Ahmet, who has brought laughter and sunshine back into my life.

In memory of Derek Staton – always my guiding North Star.

Introduction

Many people struggle with emotional eating and find that it can have an impact on their weight, their attempts to manage their weight and, just as importantly, how they feel emotionally. This workbook is intended for people who are experiencing difficulties with emotional eating and their weight. Throughout the book, I use the term "weight difficulties" to refer to the challenges associated with finding and maintaining a weight that is healthy (physically and emotionally) for you. People with weight difficulties may engage with weight-loss interventions such as lifestyle changes, medications or bariatric surgery, but it is important to address emotional eating alongside these. Emotional eating is a really common problem, particularly amongst people who have weight difficulties – for example, research tells us that approximately 60% to 70% of people who experience weight difficulties have emotional eating issues (Peneau et al., 2013; Braden et al., 2016). Furthermore, the higher a person's weight, the more likely they are to engage in emotional eating (Vasileiou & Abbott, 2023).

Why does this matter? Research tells us that emotional eating can lead to weight gain, affect a person's ability to lose weight and make it more likely that they will regain weight (Braden et al., 2016). Whilst emotional eating is an important part of the weight management picture, we are not solely interested in the effect of emotional eating on weight. Regardless of these weight difficulties, it is important to learn skills to understand and manage emotional eating because of the negative impact it can have on a person's self-esteem, their emotional health and the level of confidence they have in their ability to cope with emotions.

If you are reading this book, you may recognise that emotional eating is something that is getting in the way of how you manage your weight, how you cope with emotions and feel about yourself. Before we go further it is important to define what we mean by emotional eating and we can then figure out whether it is a significant issue for you.

What is emotional eating?

Emotional eating refers to a pattern of eating which occurs in response to specific emotions and triggers. It is often a way of managing or gaining relief from these feelings, and it is a coping mechanism that becomes an automatic habit over time. Emotional eating behaviour may involve a change in the quantity of food eaten, the type of food eaten or the way in which it is consumed. This workbook will focus on developing the skills to manage emotional eating patterns that have developed as a way of responding to, and managing, emotions – in effect, either to turn the volume up or down on emotions. For example, eating to make ourselves feel calmer or happier or to reduce difficult feelings like anxiety and sadness. In these situations, the act of eating takes on a function that is beyond the food itself.

> For me the pattern would start with a nervous butterfly feeling in my stomach and I would be thinking "I feel a bit uncomfortable and uneasy" but I would deal with that by reaching for food. The anxiety would build up across the day. I would be getting more anxious but I would be ignoring it and not thinking about why I was feeling that way. Then I would go to the shop and buy food and I'd squash that feeling. I would feel a bit sick and numb after eating. The anxiety would reduce but then that feeling would return, and the cycle would start again.
>
> *PM*

Hopefully, you can see from this quote that eating in response to emotions (emotional hunger) is different to eating in response to physical hunger. With emotional eating, there is usually a trigger (we will focus on how to identify these later) that has caused an emotional reaction, and there is usually a thought process or craving for a specific food or food type. In contrast to physical hunger, emotional hunger can happen even if the person

DOI: 10.4324/9781032664354-1

has just eaten. As you can see from the quote that follows, people often find that they do not feel full or satisfied when eating for emotional reasons because it is disconnected to feelings of physical satisfaction.

> *When I was eating through physical hunger, I would notice the taste and be more present in that moment. When I was in an emotional state I wasn't aware of how much I was eating. I was eating until the feeling of being overwhelmed or upset went away or eating until I felt physically sick.*
>
> *DK*

This workbook will focus on emotional eating, which is triggered by challenging (often perceived as negative) emotions. Although we know that it is also common for people to eat in response to "positive" emotions, there is no strong evidence that eating in response to positive emotions impacts on weight (Braden et al., 2018). The most common emotions that trigger eating are low mood, stress, and anxiety. This workbook contains exercises that will help you identify which specific emotions trigger your emotional eating.

How common is emotional eating?

Emotional eating is a very common pattern and is socially encouraged – for example, it is common for adverts and films to show people eating ice cream or chocolate to cope with a tough day. There is a spectrum of emotional eating where at one end, it is socially encouraged and a regular part of life (e.g. eating more at celebrations), but at the other extreme, it can be problematic and distressing especially when people rely on it to manage their emotions. It is the latter end of the spectrum that we will focus on addressing in this workbook. We know that emotional eating is more likely to occur amongst people living with weight difficulties (although we can't disentangle whether emotional eating causes weight issues or whether weight issues cause emotional eating) and that it impacts an individual's experience of trying to manage their weight.

Research has shown that when people eat in response to their negative or challenging emotions, they tend to choose foods that are energy-dense and hyper-palatable – this means they tend to eat foods that are high in sugar, fat and calories (Elfhag & Rossner, 2005). They are more likely to eat fast food and snack foods as well (Camilleri et al., 2014). There are also biological reasons we tend to eat more of these foods in response to emotions. For example, eating high-calorie, hyper-palatable food leads to a reduction in stress and the release of a brain chemical, dopamine, which is associated with reward (Finch et al., 2019). This is called hedonic eating and is related to the parts of the brain associated with reward and pleasure – some people have a much more exaggerated response to foods that have a high "hedonic rating", and their brains seem to practically light up! It is no wonder that they might use eating as a strategy when feeling distressed. The temporary positive feeling that people experience after eating these foods tends to strengthen or reinforce the pattern for next time they experience a difficult emotion.

To what extent are you an emotional eater?

	Not at all	A little bit	Somewhat	A lot	A great deal
To what extent do your emotions or your emotional state impact on your eating?					
To what extent does emotional eating affect your weight?					
To what extent does emotional eating impact your confidence to manage your weight?					
To what extent do you struggle to manage your emotions without eating?					
How distressed are you by your emotional eating?					
How much of a problem is emotional eating for you?					
To what extent do you feel that emotional eating stops you from achieving your goals and doing the things that matter in your life?					
How frequently do you eat as a reaction to your emotions?	1 x per month or less	2 x per month	1 x per week	2+ x per week	Daily or almost daily

There is no definite threshold or cut-off score for determining if emotional eating is a significant problem (in reality, it is your personal decision to decide if you feel that your emotional eating is a problem in your life). However, I would suggest that if your responses to three or more of the questions are in the shaded grey boxes, then this would indicate emotional eating is an important pattern to address.

When is emotional eating a problem?

We all have a unique relationship with food, and as mentioned earlier, most of us fall somewhere on a spectrum of emotional eating. For example, most people eat more than usual or eat different foods during certain celebrations or on holiday or use food as a celebration or reward. However, emotional eating becomes a problem when it:

- interferes with our attempts to manage weight and health, which then affects our functioning and causes distress,
- is our main way of coping with emotional difficulties,
- causes psychological distress.

A painful but familiar vicious cycle

Emotional eating may have developed as a coping strategy, but it often creates a different set of problems. People often describe feeling trapped in a vicious cycle whereby their emotions affect their eating which then affects their weight . . . but then their weight may affect their self-esteem and mood, which then leads to emotional eating, and so the cycle continues. The emotional eating triangle pictured (Figure 1.1) shows how these different components affect each other and lead to the feeling of being trapped in a never-ending cycle. It is important to note the two-way relationships (hence the double-ended arrows) between the different aspects – for example, emotional eating impacts weight, but weight also impacts emotional eating. Feeling distressed affects emotional eating, but the act of emotional eating leads to more distress.

Emotional eating can contribute to weight problems, but also the experience of living with weight issues and the shame, self-criticism and emotional distress that often come with this, makes emotional eating more likely to happen too. If someone has learned that eating is a way of managing difficult emotions, then they may rely on this as a coping mechanism when those emotions arise. As you can see from the variation in the quotes that follow, there is not always the same entry point - people can enter the triangle through any of the "points" and then get trapped in the cycle.

> *I think the emotional eating came from feeling overwhelmed by my weight and how I looked. If I was having a bad day thinking about my weight issues, then my natural instinct was to turn to food to soothe those feelings. Food was my soother from an emotional side but then I wasn't addressing the emotions - I was just masking or numbing them. I would eat in order to stop the negative thoughts . . . but then after you stop eating, the thoughts come back and you start beating yourself up and you become the bully in your head and then your mood gets lower. It is such a vicious cycle . . . it can feel like you are trapped.*
>
> *DK*

> *I would get upset about my weight and then I would eat because I was sad about it and then I would feel bad about my eating and then I'd think "I'm a failure, I'm never going to sort this out" and then it would go round and round. I was really trapped and upset.*
>
> *PM*

> *Eating takes stress away and makes me happy . . . my weight was a consequence of my need for food. I was always thinking about what I could eat next . . . it felt like an addiction. It felt like the weight was a consequence - it wasn't that I was stressed about my weight, it was more that I was feeling stressed and thinking "I need food, that's the thing that is going to make me happy" and then I realised I was 25 stone and hadn't really noticed the weight gain.*
>
> *CM*

Figure 1.1 The links between emotional eating, distress and weight difficulties

In this next section, I am going to break down the emotional eating triangle to look at the different connections and interactions between emotional eating, weight concerns and emotional distress. We will focus on the links between (1) emotional eating and weight difficulties, (2) emotional distress and emotional eating and (3) weight difficulties and emotional distress.

How are emotional eating and weight linked?

Emotional eating ⬌ Weight difficulties

There are lots of studies which show that emotional eating is more common amongst people who have a higher weight (Vasileiou & Abbott, 2023). Research tells us that there are a few different ways in which emotional eating can affect weight and someone's attempts to manage their weight. I will start with the negative headlines and then end on a positive!

- Weight gain - higher levels of emotional eating consistently predict weight gain over time (Frayn & Knäuper, 2018) i.e. those that engage in emotional eating are more likely to gain weight.
- Difficulties losing weight - research has found that if someone engages in emotional eating, they are much less likely to lose weight. One study found that people who engaged in emotional eating were half as likely as non-emotional eaters to lose 10% of their weight whilst in a weight loss programme (López-Guimerà et al., 2014).
- Weight regain following weight loss - higher levels of emotional eating after weight loss treatment have been found to be associated with weight regain (Elfhag & Rossner, 2005).
- And finally, on a positive note . . . addressing emotional eating is associated with weight loss. Research has found that people who reduced their emotional eating were almost twice as likely to lose greater than 7% of their weight (Braden et al., 2016).

How are emotional distress and emotional eating linked?

Emotional distress ⬌ Emotional eating

Research shows that it is a two-way relationship between emotional distress and emotional eating, i.e. some people eat in response to difficult emotions, but this eating pattern then leads to more emotional distress (shame, blame, guilt etc.). Many studies have shown that there is a link between depression and obesity (Luppino et al., 2010), and it seems that emotional eating is the link between these, i.e. people who are depressed are more likely to emotionally eat, and this is often associated with higher weight (Konttinen et al., 2019).

There are also clear links between stress, anxiety and emotional eating (Dakanalis et al., 2023), which is highlighted in the quote that follows.

> *I would feel that eating was the problem-solver at the end of a bad day. It was the thing that I knew would relieve the stress and make me happy. If I was having a bad day, I would order a takeaway and it would make everything ok. I would order enough for 3 people. It was that instant happiness and make the journey home from work exciting because I knew I had that to look forward to . . . it was just a cycle.*
>
> *CM*

When people eat in response to their emotions, it often creates a new set of psychological challenges and emotions. People often describe intense feelings of frustration, self-criticism and shame after they have engaged in emotional eating. It's one of the cruel ironies about emotional eating that the thing which people do to make themselves feel better seems to have a negative emotional effect quickly.

How are weight difficulties and emotional health linked?

Weight difficulties ◀━━━━▶ Emotional health

There are a couple of different ways in which experiencing weight difficulties impacts emotional health. As someone starts to struggle with their weight, this may have an impact on their health, which then starts to create extra challenges and places limits on what they feel able to do. As a result, people may feel unable to engage in or be excluded from activities that they might have previously enjoyed – this then starts to have an impact on mental health. Also, the embarrassment and self-consciousness that people experience about their weight has a significant effect on mood and emotional eating. People may avoid those situations where they might have to engage with people (social, work etc.) because they are fearful of judgements. In turn, this then impacts mood, and as people stay home more often, they may rely on food as a source of pleasure or a natural mood booster/anti-depressant.

Most people who struggle with their weight have tried many, many diets over the years and are often stuck in a "dieting mindset". This dieting mindset, which involves "food rules" and restriction/deprivation, can inadvertently lead to emotional eating too (Varela et al., 2019). It can be so frustrating and distressing to be trapped in this painful cycle!

Many of the issues outlined here tap into the experiences of weight stigma (either internal or external) that people experience. Weight stigma refers to the experience of feeling judged, negatively evaluated and treated differently because of weight and size. Research shows that the effect of feeling stigmatized and judged because of weight can impact eating behaviours. An important study showed that the more episodes of weight stigma that people had experienced (regardless of the degree of overweight or obesity), the more likely they were to binge-eat (Friedman et al., 2008). There is lots of evidence that feeling judged and stigmatised because of weight (either external or internal judgements) actually has the opposite of a motivating effect and is associated with increased eating and disordered eating (Carels et al., 2019). Weight stigma can also become self-directed over time-people may internalize and adopt negative societal attitudes and stereotypes about weight issues and become highly self-critical and derogatory about themselves and their weight.

A different approach to understanding emotional eating

Often, people have tried incredibly hard over many years to manage their eating through embarking on one diet followed by another, but this doesn't really address the problem of emotional eating. Learning to manage emotional eating is not simply about making eating or dietary changes, and it requires a psychological approach. I want to be clear about the fact that this workbook focuses on addressing emotional eating, not necessarily weight loss itself. This is not a "diet" book; it is a psychological skills book to help you manage emotions and thought processes that lead to eating in a way that causes distress. The approach is based on evidence-based psychological theory and strategies (primarily Cognitive Behavioural Therapy and Acceptance and Commitment therapy).

This workbook focuses on identifying and addressing psychological and emotional cues to eat. Firstly, we will focus on developing an in-depth understanding of why, and how, the emotional eating pattern started and how it continues in your current life. We will focus on understanding your emotional connections with food and how to manage your emotions rather than just focusing on changing the eating behaviour itself. In my view, the eating behaviour is a consequence of these psychological and emotional experiences, and therefore, it makes sense to focus on the cause(s), not just the consequences. In my experience, it is critical to build a solid foundation by understanding the origins of your relationship with food and the different psychological processes that keep this pattern of behaviour going. We will go through this step by step to help you build a detailed picture of your emotional eating, and this will make it much easier to then identify the most relevant and effective strategies. In effect, this is like running diagnostics on your car to identify the problem so that you can then figure out the appropriate solution rather than randomly tinkering with repairs!

But will this help me lose weight?

It is important to be transparent about the fact that managing emotional eating is just one component of the weight loss picture. My view is that by addressing emotional eating, we are removing one of the blocks which might hinder other weight loss interventions from working effectively. But perhaps more importantly, addressing emotional eating will reduce the additional feelings of frustration, blame and distress that can be really challenging and often inadvertently perpetuate emotional eating. It will also help you to develop skills in managing emotions which can be applied to other areas of your life too.

Outline of book

This book is divided into three parts, which cover different aspects of emotional eating. I will introduce a map at the start of each section, which you can use as a template to reflect your unique emotional eating patterns.

Stage 1: constructing a map of your emotional eating route

The first step focuses on building an emotional eating map and map out the "route" of your emotional eating patterns. We will identify and investigate some of the psychological processes that are landmarks and decision points along this route.

Stage 2: learning the skills to re-route and navigate emotional eating

The second step focuses on introducing new psychological skills and strategies to help you make different choices so you can exit the emotional eating route. In effect, this is where you will start experimenting with "re-routing" and developing alternative routes.

Stage 3: your future directions and map

The final step focuses on preparing for the future by developing a template. This involves consolidating the understanding that you have developed as well as the skills and strategies that are most useful for you. It also involves planning for future setbacks, as these are an inevitable part of learning to manage emotional eating.

Getting the most out of this workbook

It is important that you work through the three different stages in order, as each step builds on the previous one. Be patient! If you fast-forward or skip a step, then you won't develop the whole emotional eating map, and the approach will not be as helpful or effective. It can be tempting to fast-forward to the strategies section in the hope of finding the "answer", but the time spent developing an understanding of emotional eating and figuring out your specific patterns is crucial. I find that this process of building awareness and recognising the unique processes involved in your emotional eating (your emotional eating route) is just as powerful in creating change as the actual "strategy" work itself.

I would recommend allowing some time to focus and work through each chapter, particularly where there are exercises to complete and strategies to try out, as this will give you a chance to gather information and test things out. As with learning any new skill, it is inevitable that it will take time and practice to develop these skills and to process new information (I am sure you didn't learn to proficiently drive a car or ride a bike after your first attempt!). The book includes a range of different strategies and skills to manage emotional eating. Some will be unfamiliar, and may even feel uncomfortable, but try to have an open mind and experiment. It is inevitable that you will find some strategies more helpful than others, and some may be more applicable to your situation – just try them out so you can figure out which ones you want to carry forward and which ones you choose to put to one side.

Some final things to be aware of before you start

It is important to get some basics in place before doing more of the complex psychological work. You might also find that emotional eating is less of an issue than you originally thought after working on these foundations.

Regular eating

One of the most common eating patterns amongst people with emotional eating and weight issues is eating relatively small amounts during the day (or perhaps skipping meals) – this is problematic, though, as it leads to hunger building, and so people then often lose control of their eating in the evening. The over-eating in the evening then resets the cycle of undereating/eating irregularly during the day, as people either don't feel hungry or try to restrict their eating to compensate. Research shows that people sometimes swing from restrained to emotional eating, and this pattern is harmful and associated with higher weight (Varela et al., 2019). The lack of regular eating also impacts mood and people become much more impulsive with their choices and decisions, and this contributes to emotional eating. Regular eating is an important safety net.

Sleep

Research shows that people who have poor sleep and who do not sleep for a long duration are more at risk of emotional eating and weight issues. Research has found that if you sleep for less than 6 hours per night, this is associated with emotional eating and weight gain (Konttinen et al., 2019). If this is the case for you, then it would be helpful to consider ways of improving your sleep as part of trying to tackle your emotional eating. You should discuss any sleep difficulties with your GP, who can direct you to appropriate support.

Other weight management interventions

This workbook is suitable for people who recognise that emotional eating causes them difficulties and want to develop their understanding and skills to manage it. It is also suitable for people who want to tackle emotional eating alongside a weight loss intervention, like bariatric surgery or anti-obesity medications (e.g. GLP-1 medications). Emotional eating can be a potential obstacle to these interventions working optimally, so learning to understand and manage emotional eating is an important part of the package.

Looking after yourself whilst working through the workbook

As you are working through this workbook, you are likely to find that you become more aware of your emotions. Whilst this is positive and one of the aims of this workbook, it is important to acknowledge that you may feel unsettled and challenged at times. It is worth spending a bit of time considering who you may share these experiences with, and who is around to support you. If you find that you are feeling very distressed and/or that the process is making you aware of psychological difficulties or challenges that you were previously unaware of, then seek support from family, friends and/or healthcare professionals. Occasionally people will find that they start to identify other mental health issues (e.g. depression, trauma etc.) or disordered eating which goes beyond emotional eating (e.g. restrictive eating, bulimia), and it is important to seek help to address these via your healthcare provider.

Now that you have a bit more background information on emotional eating, let's move on to start developing and building an understanding of your specific emotional eating pattern. In the next section, I will introduce you to the emotional eating route, which is the framework that we are going to use to develop this insight.

References

Braden, A., Flatt, S. W., Boutelle, K. N., Strong, D., Sherwood, N. E., & Rock., C. L. (2016). Emotional eating is associated with weight loss success among adults enrolled in a weight loss program. *Journal of Behavioral Medicine, 39*, 727-732.

Braden, A., Musher-Eizenman, D., Watford, T., & Emley, E. (2018). Eating when depressed, bored or happy: Are emotional eating types associated with unique psychological and physical health correlates? *Appetite, 125*, 410-417.

Camilleri, G. M., Méjean, C., Kesse-Guyot, E., Andreeva, V. A., Bellisle, F., Hercberg, S., & Péneau, S. (2014). The associations between emotional eating and consumption of energy-dense snack foods are modified by sex and depressive symptomatology. *Journal of Nutrition, 144*(8), 1264-1273.

Carels, R. A., Hlavka, R., Selensky, J. C., Solar, C., Rossi, J., & Miller, J. C. (2019). A daily diary study of internalised weight bias and its psychological, eating and exercise correlates. *Psychology & Health, 34*(3), 306-320.

Dakanalis, A., Mentzelou, M., Papadopoulou, S. K., Papandreou, D., Spanoudaki, M., Vasios, G. K., Pavlidou, E., Mantzorou, M., & Giagin, C. (2023). The association of emotional eating with overweight/obesity, depression, anxiety/stress, and dietary patterns: A review of the current clinical evidence. *Nutrients, 15*(5), 1173.

Elfhag, K., & Rossner, S. (2005). Who succeeds in maintaining weight loss? A conceptual review of factors associated with weight loss maintenance and weight regain. *Obesity Reviews, 6*, 67-85.

Finch, L., Tiongco-Hofschneider, L., & Tomiyama, A. J. (2019). Stress-induced eating dampens physiological and behavioral stress responses. In *Nutrition in the prevention and treatment of abdominal obesity* (pp. 175-187). Elsevier.

Frayn, M., & Knäuper, B. (2018). Emotional eating and weight in adults: A review. *Current Psychology, 37*, 924-933.

Friedman, K., Ashmore, J. A., & Applegate, K. A. (2008). Recent experiences of weight-based stigmatization in a weight loss surgery population: Psychological and behavioral correlates. *Obesity, 16*(2), 69-74.

Konttinen, H., van Strien, T., Mannisto, S., Jousilahti, P., & Haukkala, A. (2019). Depression, emotional eating and longterm weight changes: A population-based prospective study. *International Journal of Behavioural Nutrition and Physical Activity, 16*, Article 28.

López-Guimerà, G., Dashti, H. S., Smith, C. E., Sánchez-Carracedo, D., Ordovas, J. M., & Garaulet, M. (2014). CLOCK 3111 T/C SNP interacts with emotional eating behavior for weight-loss in a Mediterranean population. *PLoS One, 9*(6), e99152.

Luppino, F. S., de Wit, L. M., Bouvy, P. F., Stijnen, T., Culipers, P., Penninx, B. W. J. H., & Zitman, F. G. (2010). Overweight, obesity, and depression: A systematic review and meta-analysis of longitudinal studies. *Archives of General Psychiatry, 67*(3), 220-229.

Peneau, S., Ménard, E., & Méjean, C. (2013). Sex and dieting modify the association between emotional eating and weight status. *The American Journal of Clinical Nutrition, 97*, 1307-1313.

Varela, C., Andres, A., & Saldana, C. (2019). The behavioral pathway model to overweight and obesity: Coping strategies, eating behaviors and body mass index. *Eating and Weight Disorders – Studies on Anorexia, Bulimia and Obesity*. https://doi.org/10.1007/s40519-019-00760-2

Vasileiou, V., & Abbott, S. (2023). Emotional eating among adults with healthy weight, overweight and obesity: A systematic review and meta-analysis. *Journal of Human Nutrition and Dietetics, 36*(5), 1922-1930.

Section 1
Understand

Introducing the emotional eating map

I want to start by introducing you to the emotional eating map which we are going to use as a template to build your understanding of your emotional eating. We will use this map to plot your automatic emotional eating route and use this as a template to identify possible exits and alternative routes.

In this next section, I am going to talk about maps, journeys and routes, so bear with me I promise it does relate to emotional eating! If the following analogy of a map doesn't fit for you, then don't worry about the language. This book will still help guide you in understanding, identifying and changing your emotional eating.

I want you to imagine your emotional eating pattern as being like a familiar, habitual route that you regularly take. We all have regular journeys that we make, and because they are become so familiar, we often tend to make these journeys on autopilot - we don't really think about the decisions or choices or notice the landmarks along the way. However, if you think about the first time you make a journey, you might use a navigation system to create the route and actively check your whereabouts and progress. With repetition and without really noticing, your brain would have automatically learned the route until it became familiar and routine. Perhaps, like me, you will have had the experience of arriving in a certain place without being completely clear about how you got there!

You might be wondering what this has to do with emotional eating. We can use this as a metaphor to describe emotional eating - i.e. there is an established and well-trodden route that you take when you experience a trigger with all sorts of processes, reactions and decisions that happen along the way. However, as with many established routes we take, we are often tuned out and don't notice these, as shown in the quote that follows. Our brains have learnt to build and follow an automatic route or pathway.

> *When you disconnect from what you are doing, you end up doing things on autopilot.*
> *I go through the same pattern every time. It is almost without fail that something happens, I feel bad . . . and then instead of dealing with the emotion or doing something else, I'll get up and go and eat something quickly. It takes the sting away from the original problem.*
>
> *PFM*

In the first part of this workbook, we will focus on identifying and mapping out the familiar and automatic emotional eating route that you take and identify where it typically ends. The endpoint is often not our intended destination; it is just the typical place that we end up, like a default option or well-trodden path. This unintended endpoint is the final, usually really painful, part of the emotional eating route where people often feel regretful or out of control of their eating, weight and/or emotions. It is the part of the vicious cycle that follows the very temporary, fleeting moments of pleasure, enjoyment or relief that come from eating.

Recognising your automatic emotional eating route

The emotional eating route will look slightly different for each person - a bit like your signature. It will be unique to you as it reflects your experiences and your reactions. In Chapter 3, we will identify and raise awareness of the typical "landmarks" along the familiar route. These are shown on the emotional eating

DOI: 10.4324/9781032664354-3

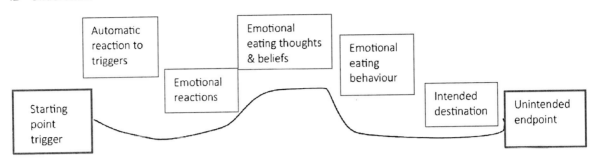

Figure 1a.1 The automatic emotional eating route

route above. This involves identifying triggers, specific emotions which relate to eating, thoughts, decisions and beliefs about food and eating as well as the features of the emotional eating behaviour itself. We will also identify the unintended endpoint of your emotional eating route. These experiences are often outside of our awareness, so by raising your awareness, we have a lot more scope to make different choices, develop new skills and influence our destination. I really want to emphasise the importance of increasing your awareness of the emotional eating route as an important step towards creating change. In my experience, this is often one of the most significant parts of the picture.

How did you learn and develop the emotional eating route?

In Chapter 2, we will rewind to look at how the emotional eating route was created and the "background learning" and processes that now influence your emotional eating. This involves thinking about your early experiences involving food, weight and emotions, identifying connections that were made between food and mood and how beliefs about emotional eating formed. I realise that the ideas and concepts that I have just mentioned may not mean very much to you now, but don't worry; we will explore each of these in detail. In my experience, this process of rewinding really matters because these background experiences and learning are likely to be directing and driving you down the emotional eating route in your present life. It helps us to understand how the behaviours we are struggling with in the here-and-now (that often cause such frustration and pain) made sense and may have even helped at some point in our lives. This is an important step in building compassion and challenging self-blame.

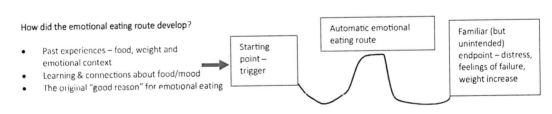

Figure 1a.2 How did the emotional eating route develop?

Where is the familiar endpoint of your automatic emotional eating route?

There is an important distinction between a destination and an endpoint. This might seem like semantics, but it is relevant to the emotional eating route. A destination is usually a place that you navigate towards with a specific intent, whereas an endpoint is a place where you might unintentionally end up. If we apply this to the emotional eating route, people are often aiming for a particular destination because of the short-term benefit or compelling reason that drives the eating, e.g. the pleasure, reward, distraction. In reality, this is a temporary pitstop, not an actual destination! The place where the emotional eating route ends - the unintended endpoint - is where people usually experience the negative consequences of emotional eating, e.g. feelings of regret, guilt, distress about weight etc. Hopefully, it is clear that there is a difference between where we aim to get to (our intended destination) and where we usually end up (the unintended endpoint).

The unintended endpoint of the emotional eating route refers to the psychological and physical consequences you may experience fairly quickly after emotional eating. Start to consider how you feel after you have emotionally eaten – what are the thoughts and feelings that arise? What do you experience after an episode of emotional eating? Here are some typical examples:

- Feeling out of control of eating
- Low self-esteem and feelings of failure
- Feeling that you have to go on a really radical diet
- Worried and fearful about dealing with emotions
- Self-critical about your weight
- Weight increases/difficulties losing weight or weight regain

An obvious fact . . . changing the route changes where you end up!

Here is a random fact: if a pilot is flying a plane, they only need to deviate by 1 degree over 60 miles to end up being significantly off course. This goes to demonstrate that small changes in a route can lead to arriving in a completely different place!

If we go back to our navigation or mapping system, there are usually lots of different exits and alternative routes that could be taken, but they are likely to be unfamiliar and possibly uncomfortable to consider currently. By starting to become aware of your automatic emotional eating route and your unintended endpoint, we can start to create some alternative routes (a bit like motorway junctions and exits, which are opportunities to take a different route) which will then change how you feel at the end of the route. I can't promise you that it will be sunshine and rainbows at your new destination, but my hope is that you will keep an open mind and judge for yourself whether it feels less distressing and more aligned with your hopes, goals and values. These may include:

- Increased sense of autonomy
- Increased ability to manage distressing emotions
- Feeling more in control (of either emotions or eating)
- Acting more in tune with self
- Feeling better about eating
- Still distressed about a life situation but not distressed about eating

It is important to be aware that at the end of your new route, you may still experience discomfort and challenges related to the original trigger, but hopefully, you won't have the added layer of the distress caused by the aftermath of the emotional eating. This often means that people have greater clarity and resources to deal with the actual problem itself.

So let's move on. In Chapter 2, we are going to focus on how the emotional eating route was originally created and constructed.

Chapter 2
Constructing a map of your emotional eating – how and why did the automatic emotional eating route develop?

In Chapter 2, we will focus on building your understanding of how the emotional eating route developed. We will consider different aspects of your early environment (your food, weight and emotional context) and how this shaped early connections between emotions and eating. Our brains learn these connections, and they become automatic and habitual. Emotional eating served a purpose at some point in your life, so we will start to identify the original "good reason" for how and why eating may have helped you to manage your emotions. This process of rewinding to understand how the past influences the present helps us make sense of why emotional eating continues despite our desire and intention to stop it in the here-and-now.

How did your emotional eating route develop?

It is important to understand how and why emotional eating patterns developed, including how emotional eating may have helped you at some points in your life and the connections that you may have made between mood and food. This section is not about blaming your past but about understanding how your emotional eating behaviours in the here-and-now (that can cause so much frustration and guilt) make sense. We need to turn towards the past to understand your eating environment, the connections you made between food and mood, and how you may have developed beliefs about eating as a positive way to respond to emotional challenges. This will help us to understand how the pathway for the emotional eating route was created. Without this unique insight and understanding, it is difficult to make meaningful changes. In my experience, this process of rewinding to look at where the pattern started has often been overlooked, as people are usually focused on trying to stop the current pattern. This step of "making sense" is a really important tool in reducing shame and frustration. I usually find that as a result of spending some time understanding the past, it makes total sense as to why the emotional eating pattern developed and why it continues.

In this next section, we are going to focus on gathering information about three areas relating to how the emotional eating route developed:

1   Your experiences and environment – We will break this down to think about the experiences and messages that you picked up in your food/eating environment, your weight/dieting environment and finally, your emotional environment.
2   Food/mood connections and learning – We will start to identify some of the links that your brain learned to make between certain emotions and eating.
3   Emotional eating beliefs – We will start to identify your early underlying beliefs about the purpose of eating as a way of managing emotions.

How did your environment and your experiences influence you?

We are going to think about the eating and food environment that you grew up in as well as the emotional environment and experiences that may have shaped your emotional eating patterns.

DOI: 10.4324/9781032664354-4

Your early eating environment

We are surrounded by messages about how food can influence and change our emotions – for example, we talk about "comfort foods" and "indulging" in certain foods. These messages linking food and emotions come from a few different places – food manufacturers, our society and culture, media and our family environment. Food manufacturers promote messages that eating particular foods will soothe difficult or challenging emotions or elevate our mood by making us feel happy or better – for example, think about how certain confectionary products are linked to positive emotions (e.g. Celebrations chocolates), and fast food is connected with happiness (McDonald's – Happy Meals). As I mentioned in Chapter 1, there is also strong evidence that certain foods (usually ultra-processed foods) have a high hedonic rating, which means they activate the part of the brain associated with pleasure and reward – this explains why we tend to eat high-fat, high-sugar foods when feeling emotional. In all my years working in this area, I have never heard of anyone eating carrots to manage their emotions!

There are important cultural beliefs and messages about certain foods, portion sizes, leaving or "wasting" food, body image and attitudes to weight. In addition, our family environment also shapes our relationship with food and the "rules" and connections we make. For example, food can be a way of expressing love, as a reward or may have been withheld as a restriction or punishment. The quotes below demonstrate that many people with emotional eating patterns are able to trace the pattern back to childhood:

> *My emotional eating stems from childhood – my mum is an emotional eater and when I was upset she would always give me biscuits. It wasn't her fault but that's where that link came from. If I felt sad as a kid, I would have a biscuit and then I felt happier after having it . . . but really what I needed was just a hug. I think I just made that connection with food early in life.*
>
> *PM*

> *I would say it started when I was in nursery school when I was about 3 or 4. I would have meals at the nursery and snacks were a reward . . . so if you were really good or well behaved, you would get a treat. I think I started seeing food as a reward but then it also became comforting. We would have lunch just before heading home so if I'd had a difficult day and another child had upset me, I think I saw that as a way of balancing out the day's experiences. If it was a nice day, it would be a celebration to end the day or if had been difficult then it would be a comfort.*
>
> *PFM*

Reflections: describe your early food environment

- What was your early food environment like (e.g. type of meals, availability of food, eating culture etc.)?

  _____

  _____

- How might your early environment have influenced your relationship with food (also possibly your body/weight)? Was food viewed in a certain way in your family?

  _____

  _____

- What connections might you have learnt between emotions and eating?

  _____

  _____

Your weight and dieting environment

It is also important to consider your weight history and how others may have responded to your weight, as it may have played a role in the development of emotional eating patterns. These experiences may include weight bullying or stigma, being encouraged to diet by family members, feeling judged because of weight which leads to secret eating etc. The case example that follows shows how early experiences of other people focusing and commenting on weight led to feelings of shame, self-consciousness and secret-eating.

Case example

B. was put on a diet at an early age by her parents, and this led to secret eating. Her dad would make negative comments about her weight and would call her a "couch potato". She started to make comparisons with her friends at school and thought, "I shouldn't be this size". Whenever weight was mentioned at school, she would feel shame and had a strong feeling that people were looking at her. As a result of these experiences, she learnt that it was better to eat secretly to avoid attention or critical reactions from other people. She felt anxious about being around people all day, and so she would eat "forbidden" foods in her bedroom and feel relaxed and safe. She also concluded that she had to lose weight for other people to approve or be proud of her and so would have periods of not eating much during the day, which would then lead to her hunger building and losing control of her eating later.

Reflections: describe your early weight and dieting environment

- What experiences did you have of others noticing or responding to your weight?

  _____

  _____

- What sort of comments did you experience about your weight? Did you experience any weight bullying?

  _____

  _____

- When did someone first mention your weight to you? Who was this? And what happened?

  _____

  _____

- Were others dieting around you? What was your "weight" environment like – were your family a similar weight or different? And how did your weight fit in?

  _____

  _____

- How did the above experiences impact your eating?

  _____

  _____

Your emotional environment and experiences

It is also important to pay attention to the emotional environment that you grew up in, as this will have shaped your experience and understanding of emotions. So, for example, if you grew up in an environment where emotional expression was actively discouraged, this will have impacted your response when strong emotions arose. Our emotional environment also affects our beliefs about how others will respond to our emotional needs too (e.g. our beliefs about how others may respond to our distress). It is inevitable that each of us will have experienced emotional challenges and stressors at various points in our lives, and it can be useful to identify if any of these experiences triggered emotional eating as a coping mechanism. A whole range of experiences may come to mind - some may be about wider family life, family difficulties, parental issues, bullying, abusive experiences, bereavements, school problems etc.

Reflections: describe your early emotional environment and experiences

- We all experience various challenges growing up – can you identify any particular issues that you feel impacted on you emotionally? How did you navigate through these issues? Did you have someone to support you?

  _____

  _____

- How did you express your emotions? How did others respond to your emotions?

  _____

  _____

- What were you taught about emotions? How did the people close to you express their emotions?

  _____

  _____

- How did food help you to manage any challenging emotional experiences (help you to "get on" with things?) How did it help you function?

  _____

  _____

What connections between food and mood did your brain learn?

The experiences that you identified will have shaped your emotional relationship with food. This connection between mood and food gets strengthened by repetition.

Our brains are designed to learn, and so we are programmed to make associations and connections – our super-keen brain recognises that Situation A goes with Situation B and then X happens. This is incredibly useful, as it means that we can take mental shortcuts and save brainpower, so we are free to use our brain resources to focus on other things. However, it can backfire on us! Our experiences and environment (both emotional and eating) lead to us making connections and shortcuts between events/situations, emotions and eating. Let me show you how it works.

Example 1

Imagine that a child is upset and crying and they are given sweets to distract them and make them feel better. Obviously, this isn't really going to have a lasting impact if it is a rare experience, but if this behaviour is repeated over time and sweets are regularly given in response to distress, then the child will learn to make a connection that when they are upset, they eat sweets, and their distress reduces. Over time, the context and circumstances are forgotten, and the emotion becomes really strongly bonded and connected with eating (so sweets are eaten in response to distress with the aim of reducing the distress).

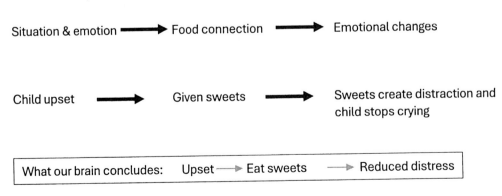

Example 2

Imagine it's the end of a tough working week. It is common for people to celebrate or reward themselves by having a takeaway on a Friday night – over time and with repetition of this behaviour, this type of food choice becomes closely connected with feelings of relief and celebration. Over time, our brains learn to make a shortcut connection between having a takeaway, reduced anxiety and reward. It therefore makes sense that next time we are in a difficult or anxiety-provoking situation, this triggers our brain to automatically remember the association with eating a takeaway and reduced anxiety. Our brains learn these connections, and we start to build a memory bank of acting on these, which then strengthens the connection for next time the situation arises.

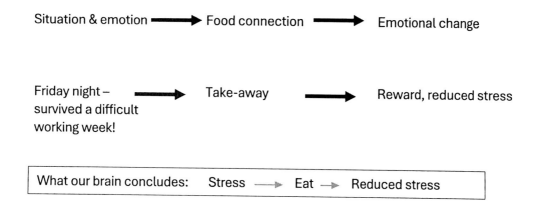

So, our brains start to create these powerful connections between specific emotions and patterns of eating behaviour. This means that when we encounter one of these tricky emotions in the future, our brain automatically remembers that eating was previously connected with a change in these emotions, and therefore, we are automatically triggered to eat.

The learning we have discussed so far, relates to what we pick up from our external environment – in other words, the early associations and connections between situations, food and mood that occur in response to certain people, our environment and life events and circumstances. However, over time, we learn to internalise these mood and food associations. This means that the actual situation or context is no longer so important as the link between the emotion and eating has become so strong and powerful.

I grew up in a volatile home and never knew what mood my Dad would be in or what the next row would be. When your external environment is uncertain, one of the things you can control is how you feel in yourself . . . I tend to feel my feelings in my tummy so when I ate, I would feel warm, safe as well as grounded and secure. The more volatile the environment was, the more I would use food to feel safe and grounded. The stress eating pattern then continued through life so even though the environment was different, and things were no longer volatile . . . when I went into a stressful job and felt anxious, food was still my way of calming myself back down and grounding myself.

DJ

The preceding quote highlights how a volatile environment led to a connection between anxiety and eating forming. However, over time, this person's belief that "eating in response to stress creates calmness and security" has been applied to a wider range of difficult or challenging situations. It is worth noting that as a child, she was obviously being very adaptive and finding a helpful way of soothing herself in a difficult environment, but this is less helpful as an adult because she now has more control of her environment and access to different resources.

Use the questions below as a prompt to reflect on your history of emotional eating and the connections between food and mood that you made.

How and when did you start to make emotional eating connections?

- Where can you trace your pattern of emotional eating back to? When do you remember first starting to eat in response to emotions? How old were you?

  _____

  _____

- What was happening around that time? Were there any life events, important changes or circumstances?

  _____

  _____

- Try to remember and describe the initial pattern of emotional eating. What would be the usual triggers? What emotions related to it? What foods would you eat? Would you be in a particular place? Did you eat secretly? What changes in your emotions did eating create?

  _____

  _____

What beliefs did you develop about how eating helps to manage your emotions?

Emotional eating served a purpose and was a problem-solving strategy

These old associations and patterns often reflect a primitive or simplistic way of trying to solve an emotional problem (our problem-solving skills tend not to be very sophisticated when we are young!). And don't forget that emotional eating is a very effective option, at least in the short term. It is highly likely that emotional eating did have a valid function or purpose at some point in your life, but most people are easily able to recognise that it no longer fulfils this purpose and seems to create more problems than it solves. Many of the people I work with who have emotional eating patterns describe feeling ashamed and confused about why they continue to do something that they *know* causes problems. There is a clash or battle between our "emotional brains" and our "rational/logical brain".

We can be pulled in different directions by the two opposing forces of our emotional brain and our rational/logical brain. We are trying to meet our emotional needs – these are based on primitive reactions driven by the "alarm system" (our brains developed to alert us to danger and protect us from harm). However, we have evolved to have a "rational/logical brain" which has higher functions of thinking, reasoning, planning, reflecting and imagining, and whilst this clearly has some obvious benefits, it can sometimes clash with the needs and drives of the "emotional brain". The emotional brain may be trying to satisfy our primitive need to escape from what we perceive to be a threatening or frightening situation, whereas the rational/logical brain may be wanting to lose weight or eat differently. This conflict reflects our competing demands and needs. This is why people often describe a temporary emotional benefit from emotional eating (the emotional brain is satisfied), which is quickly replaced by negative reactions (rational brain is dissatisfied). There is a clash between the part of the brain that wants to fire-fight our emotions versus the other part which can visualise our future hopes and goals.

What did your brain learn to conclude about how food helps with emotions?

Now that we have a sense of your history, experiences and the type of mood/food connections that formed, we can start to identify the beliefs that you developed about how eating helped you to cope and manage your emotions. By identifying these original beliefs about the function and purpose of eating in response to emotions, we can gain insight into what may be driving some of the current patterns. There is always an original "good reason" for a behaviour if we look for it. Identifying the original "good reason" shines a spotlight on the short-term driver for emotional eating, i.e. the temporary pleasure or emotional boost it might give. For example, at an earlier point in your life, if you learned to make a connection between eating in response to anxiety and concluded that eating is a way of stopping anxious thoughts, then it makes total sense that you would continue to repeat that pattern. It could also be possible that the original "good reason" was provided by a well-meaning adult who struggled to find other ways to meet your emotional needs and identified that food was a way of being able to do this in the short term.

These beliefs are likely to be out of your awareness because they will have formed at a much earlier point in your life, and we therefore tend not to be aware of them or question them. The quotes that follow highlight the underlying psychological function of emotional eating.

I had a strict childhood in terms of food and there was lots of talk about weight and dieting. Foods were labelled as "good" and "bad". When I had a feeling of being overwhelmed or I wanted to lift my mood I would turn to the "bad" foods because I felt like if I could make choices about what I ate, then I would feel more in control of the situation and somehow that I had taken control of my emotions. Eating what I wanted was a way of feeling that I was taking control, even if it didn't actually do anything to address the emotion.

DK

In the preceding example, the underlying "good reason" for emotional eating was that it created a feeling of being more in control of situations and emotions.

Food became my main source of pleasure and enjoyment. I think I've always been anxious about work and wanting to be successful and gain approval. I guess food was the thing that was a release for me. I never took time off, I worked late . . . I gave 100% . . . and food was where I could "let go". Every meal had to be really extravagant. There were no "normal" meals . . . I was eating what I really wanted and the most indulgent thing I could find, because that was the thing that was going to make me feel better.

CM

The underlying "good reason" in this example was that eating provided a release or freedom from the stress of continually seeking approval.

I grew up believing that negative emotions are basically bad - in my family, you weren't allowed to express them. A lot of effort went into masking my emotions. It was best to keep your mouth shut so I pretended to be happy all the time because that was safer. Everyone would be shouting and I would be quiet as there was a fear of making it worse. So I stood there and became numb. I'm still creating that feeling with food. That numbness and disconnect was a way of protecting me from hurt and that's what I'm managing to do that with food. Being numb is what I know. It's safer that way. It's a behaviour that I return to for the same reasons.

BJ

The underlying "good reason" in this example was a belief that feeling numb and disconnected was protective and that food was an effective means to create that feeling.

The exercise that follows will help you to start the process of identifying your original "good reason" for emotional eating.

Exercise

If you cast your mind back to some of the early experiences you identified in the previous exercise, how did emotional eating help you back then? What was your original good reason? What was the motive for emotional eating? What were the beliefs that you formed about how eating helped you manage your emotions?

You might want to think about what did eating give you? What did it take away? Try to listen to the messages you have sent to yourself.

- When I feel X, eating xxx makes me feel xxx.

- Eating allows me to . . .

- If I eat X, it makes me feel xxx.

- If I eat X, the feeling of X increases.

- If I eat X, the feeling of Y reduces.

- If I want to feel Y, then eating X creates that.

Don't worry if you find it difficult to identify your "initial good reason" at this point – this can be tricky at first, and we will continue to build on these ideas throughout the book. Hopefully, you can at least take comfort from the fact that you are not alone in struggling with this and that the initial intention driving the emotional eating had a rational basis and was an attempt to solve a problem.

Summary of how and why your emotional eating route developed

In this next section, we will start to pull together some of the information about how your brain learned to make emotional eating connections and the emotional eating beliefs that developed. It takes time to reflect, so don't be concerned if things aren't falling into place yet. The main thing at this stage is just to be open and curious about how these patterns and connections may have formed.

I will show you a case study example of how an emotional eating route developed so that you can start to see the connections and beliefs that formed.

Experiences and environment

- Mum always on a diet – no "treat" foods allowed at home (message given that weight needs to be "managed")
- Would eat "treat" foods in secret on the way home from school with sister
- Bullied at school and was home-schooled – would feel depressed at home and would eat

Connections and learning

"Treats" are "bad" and must be eaten in secret.
Sweets and snacks make me feel better emotionally.

Emotional eating beliefs/the original "good reason"

Eating certain foods gives me pleasure/joy.
Eating "treat" foods makes me feel temporarily in control.

In the following exercise, see if you can start to bring together some of the information we have identified in this chapter about how and why your emotional eating route developed.

 Exercise

Experiences and environment
What experiences impacted the development of your emotional eating pattern?

Connections and learning
What connections and associations did you make between food and mood?

Beliefs and original "good reason":
What emotional eating beliefs formed? With hindsight, what do you recognise as the original "good reason"?

How do these past experiences link to the present?

Our past experiences and learning lay the foundations for our reactions to current situations. We all have unique vulnerabilities or "hot spots" based on our past experiences which, when "triggered", will influence our reactions in the here-and-now. In the next chapter, we will start to identify some of the situations or circumstances which trigger your emotional eating. Often, we find that there is a theme or pattern around triggers, as they tend to cluster around situations which activate certain thought processes or feelings. We will do more work on this in Chapter 3, but I just wanted to highlight this important connection between the past and present.

Key points and tasks:

- Our past experiences and early environment influence our relationship with food, weight and our emotions.
- Our brains are wired to make and learn connections – in this scenario, between situations, emotions and food. Over time and with repetition, we make strong, automatic connections between mood and food, and we develop beliefs about how eating helps our emotional state. This becomes the original "good reason" for emotional eating. Emotional eating served a purpose at some point in our lives, but we don't necessarily update these beliefs or connections, so we just keep on repeating the same behaviour, regardless of whether it works effectively now.
- You can continue to build and work on the following tasks:

  - Reflecting on past experiences and your environment and how this impacted your emotions and eating.
  - Connections that you made between certain situations, emotions and eating (remember that the link between emotions and eating will have become stronger over time).
  - Identifying your original "good reason", as this forms the basis for your emotional eating beliefs.

- What is the next step? The next step is to start to gather more information and detail about the choices and landmarks on your emotional eating route.

Chapter 3
Constructing a map of your emotional eating
Recognising your automatic and familiar emotional eating route

In this next chapter, we will gather more information about the various psychological processes, landmarks and decision points on your automatic emotional eating route. We will work through various exercises to help you identify your triggers, your reactions to triggers and the specific emotions and thought processes which influence emotional eating. We will also identify the differences between your intended destination and unintended endpoint on the emotional eating route.

Mapping out your automatic and familiar emotional eating route

In the last chapter, we focused on how associations and connections between mood and food develop. These past connections have a "priming" effect, which explains how and why emotional eating gets triggered or activated in the present day. In this section, we are going to investigate your current emotional eating patterns by gathering information on the automatic emotional eating route that you take. Identifying the route is an important strategy because then you can step back and recognise when it is happening, rather than just blindly following it. This means that ultimately, you can make some different choices and use new skills. Whilst there is a familiar emotional eating route that occurs in response to triggers, you will soon learn that there are many different psychological processes involved. There is a pattern of responding in a certain way to triggers, which then leads to emotional reactions, which then activate thoughts and beliefs about emotional eating, which then drives the eating behaviour. Once you start thinking about it, it is surprising how many steps or processes are involved in emotional eating! In this next section, we will start to gather specific information about these different "landmarks" along the route shown. Often people have focused their attention on the actual eating behaviour, not these other aspects. When we become more aware of these, there are many more opportunities and options for change along the way.

By following these next steps, you will start to build a detailed understanding of:

- Your triggers for emotional eating
- The thoughts and interpretations that influence your reaction to a trigger
- The specific emotions connected with emotional eating and your reaction to these emotions
- Your emotional eating thoughts and beliefs
- Features of your emotional eating behaviour
- Your intended destination and unintended endpoint

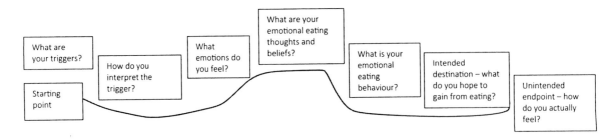

Figure 3.1 Mapping out the emotional eating route

DOI: 10.4324/9781032664354-5

Emotional Eating Diary – complete when you notice that you have eaten for emotional reasons

Day/time	What was the trigger? (event, physical feeling, place etc)	Reaction to the trigger – what did you think about it? What were you saying to yourself?	Emotions – can you identify and label the emotion(s) you experienced?	Emotional eating thoughts – when you were feeling X emotion, what thoughts about food went through your mind?	Behaviour – what did you do? Did you eat?	How did you feel afterwards? Short-term Longer-term

Figure 3.2 Emotional eating diary

Tracking emotional eating – recognising your route markers

As mentioned earlier, we aren't going to focus on *what* you are eating; the aim is to focus on what happens before you engage in emotional eating behaviour to help us identify and develop alternative options. We will go through each section in the rest of this chapter, but I just want to introduce you to an emotional eating diary at this point so you can hold the framework in mind when you are reading through the following sections.

This is just one version of an emotional eating diary. You can use this as a template, but feel free to adapt it. You might find that there are some parts which are more difficult to fill in, but don't worry; it will become easier over time as you start to tune in. The principle is to step back and notice the pattern of your triggers, self-talk, feelings and behaviour, and you can do this in whichever format works for you. Some people prefer to fill in a form, or some prefer to use the headings to make written notes or notes on their phone. Although it can be tempting to rush into making lots of changes, it is better to just be curious and notice what is happening now. These are important steps in building awareness of your automatic emotional eating route, and this recognition is an important part of change.

Identifying triggers: what is your starting point?

We will start by identifying the triggers for emotional eating. Triggers can be internal (e.g. a physical feeling) or external (e.g. related to a situation, relationship, finances etc.). The way we react to these triggers creates a domino effect, whereby the reaction affects our emotions and then our eating.

By identifying the triggers for emotional eating, you will start to recognise a pattern which will help you be more prepared in future and notice when it is happening in real time. This awareness and recognition creates distance from the situation – almost as though you are hovering above, observing and watching rather than being "in" the situation. This process will make it easier for you to slow down. We can't necessarily eliminate triggers, but we can learn to prepare, navigate and re-route around them – a bit like spotting a hazard ahead when you are driving.

Often, people tend not to pay a lot of attention to the actual trigger itself because they are focused on dealing with the emotional consequences of it, i.e. eating to manage how they feel about it. The emotional eating then leads to a spiral of shame and guilt and activates the dieting mindset, which takes the focus even further away from noticing and responding differently to the original trigger. The idea is that by identifying triggers, we can think about some opportunities for change much earlier in the process.

Triggers can be external or internal and can relate to situations or circumstances, physical feelings, our thoughts, our mood etc. Sometimes, people describe an emotion as being a trigger, but emotions are usually a reaction or consequence of something else, even if it can be tricky to identify exactly what this is. Usually, I find that if you look closely enough at what preceded the emotion, there is a trigger that has caused the emotion.

At first, you may find that it is easier to tune into the changes in your emotions rather than what has caused the change. You can use these shifts and changes in your emotions as a prompt to rewind and tune in to what was happening before. Where were you? What happened? Who were you with?

The list that follows includes some common emotional eating triggers:

- Situation, e.g. work, argument
- Particular thought pattern (e.g. I can't cope.)
- Upsetting comment
- Reminder of weight
- Worry about future event
- Life stress
- Contact with a particular person or challenging relationship
- Physical feeling, e.g. tiredness, pain
- Memory or loss/bereavement
- Particular places, e.g. on the sofa in the evening

What are your typical triggers? What happens before you emotionally eat?

1

2

3

4

5

It is likely that after you have monitored your triggers for a while, you will start to notice some repetition and similarities. For now, your role is simply to notice the triggers with curiosity and without judgement, and then in Chapter 4, we will think about what you can do to manage and respond differently to them.

What happens in your mind when you experience a trigger?

Once you have experienced a situation that is triggering for you, how do you respond and react? You might have noticed on the emotional eating map at the start of the chapter that identifying our interpretation of the trigger (our self-talk and thought processes) is an important part of the emotional eating process. This is because our internal conversation and the thoughts we have when we encounter a trigger often drive our emotional reaction, and this, in turn, drives our eating behaviour.

Try to picture your mind as being like a filter or lens through which you experience and interpret triggers. The idea is that if you put different people in the same situation, they will each have a different view or perspective on the situation, and this will lead to different emotional reactions. So, for example, if a friend didn't call when they said they would, then Person A may think, "They are completely unreliable and don't care about me" and feel angry and sad. Person B, in the same situation, may have the following interpretation: "They have got lots on at the moment and it just slipped their mind to call", which left them feeling neutral. So, when people encounter a trigger, the type of interpretation or internal conversation they have about the trigger then drives the emotional reaction that follows.

Following are some other examples which show how a person's unique interpretation and self-talk in response to a trigger then drives their emotional reaction.

Trigger ⟶	Interpretation, thought processes and self-talk related to the ⟶ trigger	Emotional reaction
Demands on time	I've got no time for anything. Why do I have to sort everyone else out? There's no time for me.	Stressed, overwhelmed
Pain	I can't cope with feeling this way. It is taking over my life.	Sad, hopeless

Why is it important to become more aware of our thoughts and interpretations? This is because they become automatic and repetitive (like habits) and usually go unquestioned, yet they are really powerful because they drive our emotions (and behaviour). The idea is that by becoming aware of your interpretations and thoughts, you can then start to notice and question them and consider if they are serving you well (i.e. are they accurate? helpful? Do they facilitate you moving towards your goals?). By paying attention to them, we can start to notice and possibly change our thinking habits, and this, in turn, can have a knock-on effect on the emotions which then affect our eating. In Chapter 4, we will focus on developing skills to manage reactions to triggers and regain perspective, but I just wanted to flag at this point that this is not simply about changing negative thoughts into positive thoughts.

There are some useful questions that will help you identify the interpretations, self-talk and thoughts that run through your mind after encountering a trigger.

What was going through your mind?
What were you saying to yourself?
If I was able to overhear you at that moment, what would I hear you saying to yourself?

Exercise

Often, people find it easier to tune into their emotions first and then work backwards to try to figure out the "missing" thought process. You can try this out by bringing to mind the last time you were in a situation that caused an emotional reaction (e.g. stress, sadness, overwhelm etc.). Now, try to rewind and replay the situation in your mind and focus in on what you were saying to yourself. What thoughts went through your mind?

_____

_____

_____

_____

What are the specific emotions connected with eating?

So far, we have identified your triggers and reactions to these triggers which subsequently lead to an emotional reaction. Now, we are going to take this a stage further and identify the specific emotions that are linked with emotional eating.

Trigger and self-talk about ⟶ Emotional reaction to trigger ⟶ Eating
the trigger

Before we move on, just stop for a second and think about the typical way you (and others) answer when someone asks "How are you? How are you feeling?"

We may get asked this question a few times per day or week. I want you to replay in your mind how you generally respond when you get asked this question. What sort of phrases do you use? How much detail do you give? Is the question followed up, or do you move on?

If you look at the typical responses that follow, do you recognise any of your own responses?

How are you feeling?

"Fine, thanks".
"Not great".
"Yeah . . . so-so".
"Good, thanks".

This exercise is a way of demonstrating that our emotional vocabulary is often limited and restricted – we tend to use phrases that don't provide a lot of specific information. We might describe feeling "good" or feeling "bad" or just rely on stereotypical phrases. This is a problem because it doesn't really give us very much information about someone's exact emotional state. It is difficult to create a deeper understanding about a person's emotions from these descriptions. This is why in the next section, we are going to focus on identifying the specific emotions you experience, as this will help us decode the message the emotion is communicating.

Why is it important to work out the specific feelings you are experiencing?

Emotions act like signals or messages from the brain. There is a specific meaning or message attached to different emotions. Emotions are designed through evolution to act as signals to help us identify our needs and meet our goals. They have an underlying meaning that is intended to flag something to us. That is why it is important to be able to notice them, listen to them and decode the meaning of them. If you can tune in and identify the specific emotion you are experiencing, then you also then have a greater chance of figuring out what the emotion means and, therefore, what the underlying need is. This will become clearer!

We are not necessarily taught how to notice, label and listen to our emotions - it is often a new skill to learn, so don't worry if it takes time or doesn't come naturally. In fact, through our life experiences, we may have been actively encouraged to ignore our emotions - for example, if we have always had to think about other people's needs and been praised for doing that, then over time, we might have learned to ignore our own emotional needs. We might do this so much that it is challenging to suddenly start noticing and recognising emotions. Figuring out exactly what emotions you are feeling will also help you to notice and understand the trigger for these emotions. As a result of paying attention to the trigger and the emotional reaction, eating becomes a less obvious part of the picture. You are focusing your attention on the *actual* problem, not the consequence.

Working out your emotional eating signature - what are the most common emotions which impact your eating?

I am going to show you a couple of different tools that you can use to identify which specific emotions impact on your eating behaviour.

If you look at the chart of emotions that follows, you might find that you instantly recognise some of the key emotions that are typically connected with your emotional eating. The list is just a starting point to encourage you to zoom in and be more specific about which emotions impact your eating. There might be certain emotions that you experience which aren't on this list, so obviously, feel free to add these.

Inadequate	Shame	Irritated	Nervous	Hurt
Boredom	Disappointed	Annoyed	Worried	Ashamed
Disgust	Angry	Anxious	Stressed	Guilty
Empty	Mad	Scared	Overwhelmed	Down
Panicked	Helpless	Sadness	Embarrassment	Lonely
Other?	Other?	Other?	Other?	Other?

Another, more detailed way of identifying emotions is through using the feelings wheel that follows. This breaks down categories of emotions into much more detailed and specific emotions. It can be a really useful way of narrowing down exactly what you are feeling and to name highly specific emotions.

As a result of learning to identify and notice your emotions, you will hopefully be able to identify some of the typical emotions that impact your eating. Make a note of these in the space that follows.

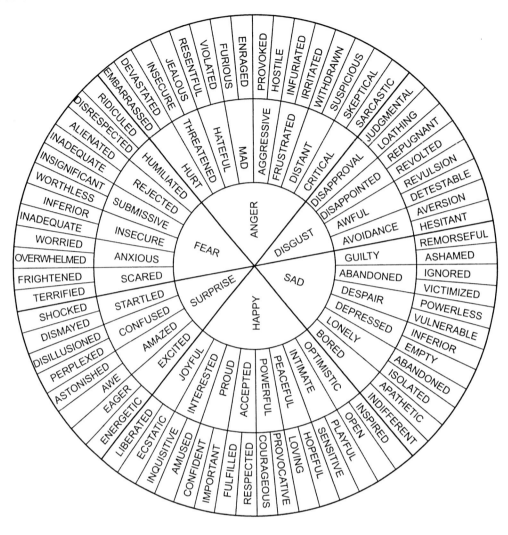

Figure 3.3 Feelings wheel

Which are the most common emotions that impact your eating?

1

2

3

4

5

Don't worry if you find it difficult to identify the specific emotions which influence your eating at this point – it will become a bit clearer as you start tracking your emotional eating patterns. For now, it is good enough that you accept that there is a wide range of emotions and start to foster some curiosity about which ones are most relevant to your eating. The process of turning your attention towards your emotions is an important step in its own right. In Chapter 5 (Exit 2), we will think in more detail about how to understand and respond differently to these emotions.

What are your emotional eating thinking patterns?

The diagram that follows shows the chain reaction of events and experiences. So far, we have worked through the process of identifying triggers, your reactions to triggers and the specific emotions you experience. The next step is to identify the emotional eating thought process which then leads to the eating behaviour. This process is not necessarily something that people are always aware of, and it can take time to tune in to the internal food/eating thoughts, decisions and choices that occur which then lead to eating. They are important though because our thoughts are the catalyst for the behaviour. To put this into context, not everyone who experiences feelings of stress or sadness eats in response to these emotions, so there must be a thought process that acts as a bridge between the difficult feeling and the eating behaviour.

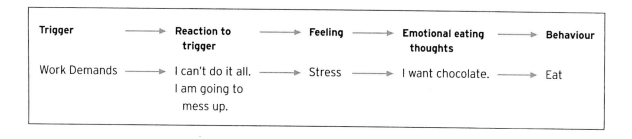

It is not quite as simple as the preceding example, though, as there are different layers and levels of thoughts, and this is where the emotional eating thought ladder comes in! At the risk of complicating things, I just want to gently introduce the different types of emotional eating thoughts to you at this point. We will spend much more time working through this in Chapter 6.

What is the emotional eating thought ladder?

There are different types of emotional eating thoughts that vary in terms of our awareness of them and how easy they are to access. The example of "I want chocolate" is one which is close to the surface, but there are plenty of other thoughts hidden beneath this one. Working from the top of the emotional eating to the bottom are:

1 Thoughts about wanting specific foods/eating (e.g. I want chocolate)
2 Decision-based thoughts to act on the original food/eating thoughts (usually giving permission or justifying).
3 Beliefs about food and mood (these are usually related to the food/mood connections and original "good reasons" we identified in Chapter 2)

The lower the rung of the ladder, the more the thoughts are out of conscious awareness.

How does this work in reality? When you experience a specific emotion, you might start to notice "surface" food or eating thoughts (often, thoughts or cravings about wanting particular foods) that are relatively easy to access. Often, once these thoughts have popped up, the person has to make a choice or decision about whether to act on them, i.e. should I have the food that I am craving? These decision-based thoughts about eating usually focus on giving permission to eat, i.e. rationalising and justifying the decision to eat. And finally, on the lowest rung of the emotional eating ladder are the underlying beliefs and associations between food and mood – these are the ones that we started to identify in Chapter 2. These are the emotional eating beliefs that developed about the positive aspects of eating as a way of coping or managing difficult emotional experiences. There are a couple of examples of emotional eating thought ladders that follow:

Example 1

Food thoughts	I want chocolate
Decision thoughts	Chocolate is a reward for getting through the day. It is something to look forward to at the end of the day when I can finally relax
Food/mood beliefs	Eating chocolate helps me relax.

Example 2

Food thoughts	I want to order a burger meal (favourite fast food) via a delivery app.
Decision thoughts	I can afford it. It will give me pleasure. It will save time, as I won't have to go out to the shops to get food for lunch then.
Food/mood beliefs	Eating junk food is a way of breaking up the grind of the day... it gives me pleasure and relieves boredom.

Figure 3.4 Emotional eating ladder

This next exercise is designed to help you notice your emotional eating thoughts.

You might find that it is difficult to notice your thoughts at first. This is completely normal and natural as it takes time to tune in. It's a bit like trying to listen to the radio when the volume is turned down low. The act of focusing your attention and listening means you will be able to pick up and hear more. Just noticing that there is a thought process and that there are different types of thoughts is a massive step forward. We will focus on the emotional eating thought ladder in more detail in Chapter 6 (Exit 3). For now, all you need to do is try and become more aware of the emotional eating thought process.

Exercise - accessing your thoughts

Choose one of the emotions that is often associated with emotional eating. Try to bring to mind the last time that you ate in response to that emotion. Where were you? What was happening? Try to get a vivid memory in your mind.

When you started to experience the emotion, what was the internal conversation that you had with yourself? What thoughts about food did you notice? What did you say to yourself that then led to eating?

_____

_____

_____

_____

What is your emotional eating behaviour?

I now want you to collect some specific information about the emotional eating behaviour itself. Emotional eating might involve a change in the quantity of food eaten, the type of food eaten or the way in which it is consumed.

Exercise

Think about the last time that you ate for emotional reasons.

What did you eat?
    Do you tend to eat specific foods when you feel this way?

How much did you eat?
    Was there a change in the amount of food that you eat?

Where did you eat?
    In secret? Away from others? In a particular room? In your car?

How did you eat?
    Does your speed of eating change?
    Were you standing, sitting, lying down whilst eating?

Is it more likely to happen at a particular time of day?

How much attention were you paying to the food as you ate?

Where do you actually end up when you follow this automatic route?

Earlier in the book, I made a distinction between your intended destination and unintended endpoint on the emotional eating route. As a reminder, the destination is the reward, pleasure, distraction that we believe that emotional eating will provide, which then motivates us and drives the behaviour. However, in reality, the destination is often somewhere that we fleetingly pass through, and we often end up in a completely different place (the unintended endpoint). So we might get the "quick fix" pleasure but usually end up experiencing negative emotional consequences (e.g. shame, guilt, frustration) or physical consequences (weight gain, fatigue, bloating etc.). There is a mismatch between what we want and what we get from the experience of emotional eating.

What is your intended destination?

Take some time to reflect on what you anticipate or hope that you will get from emotional eating in the short term by rating the following reasons in the table below. As you do this, remember that we only repeat behaviours because they served a purpose at some point in our lives, so try to avoid blaming and shaming yourself. We must acknowledge the fact that food is very effective in meeting many of our short-term needs - it is cheap, quick, readily available, may trigger feelings of pleasure, safety, contentment and triggers changes in our brains - it makes sense that we would be drawn to it.

Short-term rationale for emotional eating	Rate the extent that that this "works" in the short term: 1 = not at all, 2 = a bit, 3 = somewhat, 4 = quite a lot, 5 = extremely
Eating will provide pleasure, enjoyment	
Eating will be a distraction from difficult tasks or difficult emotions	
Eating will provide a break between activities	
Eating will provide relief from boredom	
Eating is a reward or treat to look forward to	
Eating is a way of getting specific food thoughts out of mind (quietening my mind)	
Other?	
Other?	
Other?	

What is your unintended endpoint?

As mentioned, the benefits of emotional eating are often very short-lived and quickly replaced by feelings of distress and unhappiness about this pattern of eating. There is a gap between our hopes and the reality of emotional eating. It is helpful to be specific about the exact impact that emotional eating has on you - for example, how you feel emotionally and physically, the conclusions and judgements you might make. The reason for this is that if you are clear about the current consequences (your unintended endpoint), then once you start to experiment with using some of the strategies outlined in the following section, you can start to compare and judge the impact of these. Like researchers, we want to know if the new strategy or intervention makes a difference to the outcome (how you feel). This approach involves paying attention and collecting information to help you make an informed choice about whether the approach is working and if you need to add anything else in or continue building your skills. The following list contains some of the common emotional and psychological consequences of emotional eating that people experience.

Try to recall a time when you have eaten for emotional reasons and think about the thoughts and feelings you experienced afterwards. As you reflect on your own experiences, to what extent do you identify with any of the following? Are there any additional ones that you need to add?

Longer-term consequences:	Rate the extent that you experience these emotional eating consequences: 1= not at all, 2 = a bit, 3= somewhat, 4 = quite a lot, 5 = extremely
Feeling out of control of your eating	
Feeling fearful of your emotions	
Worrying that you are dependent on food to manage your feelings	
Feeling self-critical about emotional eating as it sabotages your intention to manage your weight	
Feeling self-conscious about your weight and eating	
Feeling like you have failed	
Feeling unable to cope in ways that don't involve eating	
Feeling frustrated with yourself	
Feeling physically uncomfortable	
Noticing changes in your weight that you are unhappy about	
Other?	
Other?	

What is the next step?

By this point, you will have collected a *lot* of different information about the processes driving your emotional eating - the triggers, the way you interpret and respond to these, the typical emotions connected with your emotional eating, your emotional eating thought patterns and beliefs and characteristics of the emotional eating behaviour - as well as identifying the psychological impact of this pattern. The next step is to bring this all together to build your unique emotional eating route. This template or map of your current emotional eating patterns will reflect your new understanding of these different processes. This map is a tool for recognising the route as well as for identifying which of the strategies in the next section of the book are likely to be most relevant and helpful.

Constructing your emotional eating map

Our next step is to pull together the information that you have gathered in Chapter 2 and Chapter 3 about your emotional eating route. There is an example of a completed emotional eating route that follows and also a blank worksheet for you to start completing. Fill in what you know so far on the blank worksheet, but feel free to move things around to fit your specific circumstances so that it represents your individual emotional eating route.

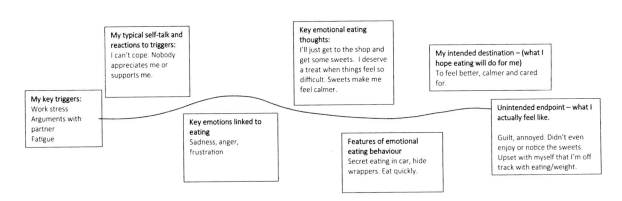

Figure 3a.1 Example of a completed emotional eating route

Reflecting on the emotional eating map – what alternatives and exits do you need?

In the next section, I am going to start introducing you to some of the skills and strategies that we will explore and test. However, before we move on to that, I want you to just take a bit of time to reflect on your current emotional eating route and consider the possibilities for change. Consider the following questions, and note down any thoughts or reflections.

If you were to step back and review what you know so far, what do you think are the options for change? What possible exits can you identify? How could you respond differently? What are the gaps in your strategies? What do you want to do differently? What skills might you need to develop? In other words, if you didn't emotionally eat, what thoughts and feelings would you have to learn to manage? What skills do you think you would need to develop to cope with the actual triggers, thoughts and feelings?

_____

_____

_____

_____

DOI: 10.4324/9781032664354-6

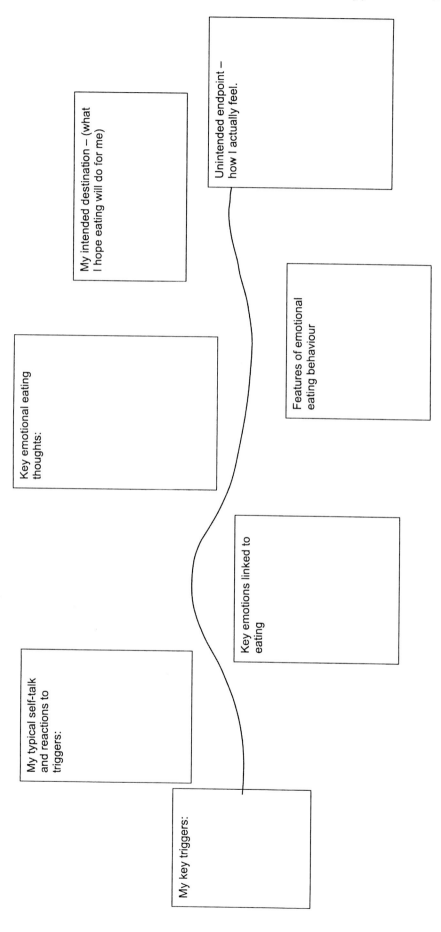

Figure 3a.2 Blank emotional eating route

Again, just to remind you that this isn't about looking for an easy, alternative swap for emotional eating – it is about developing the skills to deal with the actual drivers of the behaviour. Initially, it may be a rougher journey which requires more concentration and focus whilst you are creating the route, but there will hopefully be some satisfaction and pride in the fact that you are developing a sustainable approach which is less damaging to your emotional health. Whilst you are developing these new skills and introducing changes, the route may feel "clunky" and possibly uncomfortable. In order to feel more confident that you can manage your emotions, eating and weight, you will need to be willing to learn and experiment with new skills, based on the understanding that this will serve you better in the long run.

Section 2

Learning the skills to recognise, re-route and navigate emotional eating

Starting to build alternative routes and find new destinations

Emotional eating has often become one of the main strategies people use to manage their emotions, and the more often a behaviour is repeated, the stronger and more automatic the pattern becomes. This means that we tend to lose our flexibility and adaptability and just automatically follow the familiar route (or pathway in our brain), regardless of whether it is the most effective option for us. Over time, we develop tunnel vision so that emotional eating becomes our main strategy for coping with difficulties, and we therefore don't develop (or we forget) other ways of managing these emotions. This is why we end up in the same painful place at the end of the emotional eating route, even though we don't necessarily want or choose to be there. Through collecting the information outlined in the previous section, you should have a clearer idea of your usual emotional eating route. So now it is time to start developing some alternative routes and exits (not just travelling along on autopilot, repeating the same pattern which causes distress and unhappiness). I am not necessarily saying that the alternative route is going to be easy or comfortable, as it will involve learning to manage difficult emotions and problematic thoughts – but at least you will be dealing with the actual issue and not just adding more problems and layers of distress on top. To put it bluntly, the aim is not necessarily to get rid of distress but to avoid adding another layer to it. To do this, we must develop strategies for coping with difficult thoughts and feelings that are more effective and sustainable than eating.

Developing skills to re-route and exit from the automatic emotional eating route

In Chapter 3, we identified the unintended endpoint of the emotional eating route. Sadly, it is often one that is associated with emotional pain and distress. We are now ready to start thinking about introducing and developing different strategies that create an alternative to emotional eating and ultimately lead to a different endpoint. This involves developing new routes that lead to different destinations, so instead of having just one fixed route, you will develop more flexible routes which lead to alternative destinations.

The different skills and options that we are going to work through are listed here:

- Exit 1 – How to manage your response to triggers – building in a pause, slowing down, zooming out, keeping perspective and managing our automatic reactions.
- Exit 2 – How to understand and manage emotions directly without eating.
- Exit 3 – How to manage some of the thoughts and beliefs that might connect with emotional eating.
- Exit 4 – Identifying alternative behaviours to emotional behaviour – these include ones you can use in the moment (e.g. breathing, distraction, mindful eating) and also longer-term options which involve thinking about how you care for yourself and your body.

DOI: 10.4324/9781032664354-7

These options are shown as possible exit routes on the automatic emotional eating route that follows. To put this into context, if you develop different skills to manage your emotions, then you will be able to re-route away from your familiar emotional eating journey and proceed in a different direction (which will ultimately end up in a different place).

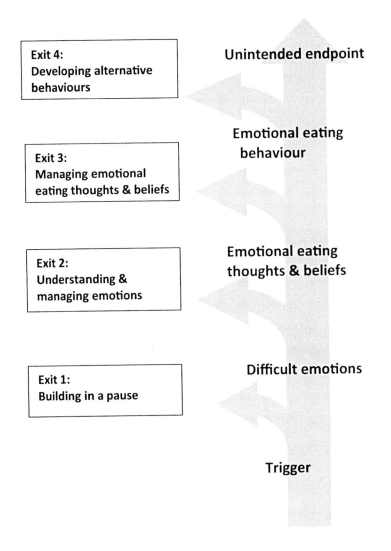

Figure 4a.1 Possible exits from the automatic emotional eating route

Are your foundations in place?

Just a couple of reminders before we get going about the importance of eating regularly and making sure that you are getting enough sleep (that is good quality), as these are fundamentals. See Chapter 1 and Chapter 7 for more information on these. Also, try to remember that it will take time to learn and practice the skills and strategies in the next stage of the book. It is useful to have a balance between having an open mind which allows you to experiment, whilst also recognising the importance of persistence and compassion whilst learning new skills.

Chapter 4
Exit 1

Responding to triggers by building in a pause and managing your reactions

This is our first exit from the familiar emotional eating route. In this chapter, we will focus on strategies to help you manage your immediate reactions to triggers. We will work through strategies to help you slow down and build in a pause so that your emotional eating reaction is less automatic. We will identify ways in which you can regain perspective by noticing and questioning your reaction so that you regain clarity and perspective.

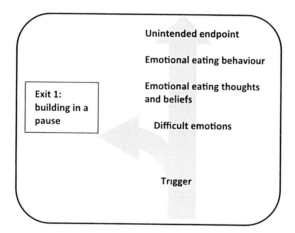

Figure 4.1 Exit 1: building in a pause

In Chapter 3, we started to identify triggers for emotional reactions which then lead to emotional eating. By this point, you will be aware that emotional eating can become like a reflex reaction to triggers and emotions. In this next section, we are going to focus on slowing down so that you can start to build in a gap between the emotion and the response.

Whilst there may be some triggers that we can avoid or influence, this is not always possible. We cannot rid life of all events or situations that might trigger an emotional reaction - life would be pretty dull and monotonous even if this was possible! However, we do have the ability to influence and make choices about how we respond to triggers. We can learn to create a gap between a trigger and how we respond. The reaction to triggers and the emotions that arise from them becomes very fast and automatic - the gap between them gets smaller and smaller over time. So, by recognising what is happening we can actively build in a pause to give the brain time to catch up and make some active choices and decisions about the most useful and helpful options. This gap allows us to consider our options and make choices and decisions that might work better for us. Remember in Chapter 2, I mentioned the different needs of the emotional brain versus the rational/logical brain? By learning to create a gap or pause after experiencing a trigger, this allows time for the rational/logical brain to catch up and get more involved in the decision-making process.

DOI: 10.4324/9781032664354-8

When you build in a pause, the brain starts to learn that when you experience a particular emotion, the response that follows isn't always eating - for example, that when you feel stressed (or another emotion), eating is not always the next step in the sequence. The brain adjusts to there being an alternative response following the emotion, and over time, this creates a new habit. This is a way of undoing past patterns and creating new connections and pathways in the brain.

Hopefully, you are starting to gain a bit of an insight into your typical triggers and whether these cluster into a certain pattern or theme. This is important because our brains have evolved to be experts at pattern recognition. Imagine that you are driving along and spot a hazard in the distance - you would slow down, think about the options, and decide the best approach. To do this, your observation skills need to be switched on. The work that you did in Chapter 2 and Chapter 3 will have helped you to "switch on" and recognise the pattern. In the next section, we are going to continue building on this.

We will first focus on observing and noticing when you encounter a trigger, learn how to build in a pause and calm the brain and then move on to explore the thought processes involved in our reaction.

Developing observation skills - watching yourself with curiosity

There are different parts of our minds - our "doing" mind, our "thinking" mind and our "feeling" mind. These are the parts that we tend to be most familiar with, but we also have a "noticing" mind. This is the part that is able to step back and observe. You can be doing something but also observing yourself doing it - like there is a part of us that is overseeing and has the full picture. Likewise, you can be experiencing an emotion (I am feeling anxious) but also noticing that you are experiencing the emotion (I am noticing that I am feeling anxious). This "noticing" part of our mind can be incredibly useful for helping us to slow down and notice automatic reactions. It's a bit like watching yourself (or hovering above yourself like a helicopter).

The "noticing" mind can help you to recognise the problematic patterns that your "doing", "thinking" and "feeling" mind gets tangled up in. It is your "noticing" mind that tells you "Aha, I recognise this scenario, and I know how this tends to play out". This is illustrated in the quote that follows.

> *Sometimes when I realise that I am emotionally eating, I do sometimes just stop and go "this isn't really what I want to do". I did it last night after a long busy day at work. We ordered a takeaway and I found myself dishing up another portion and then I looked down at my plate and thought "I don't actually want to eat this. I'm not actually hungry. I've put it there because I have had a bad day and I am worried about things to come". I decided to stop eating as I didn't want or need it and I just moved on. It takes time to learn to recognise and do this. When you disconnect from what you are doing, you end up doing things on autopilot.*
>
> *PFM*

The "noticing" mind helps you to tune in and recognise the thoughts, feelings and reactions you are experiencing and to step back from them.

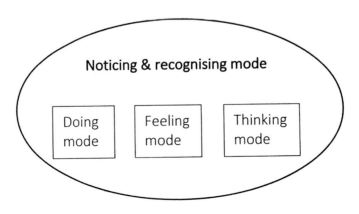

Figure 4.2 The "noticing" mind observes the "doing", "thinking" and "feeling" mind

Learning to tune in and observe

The next step involves learning to check in and notice what physical sensations, emotions and thoughts you are experiencing in the moment. The more we learn to recognise our thoughts and emotions, the earlier we can spot them and learn to respond differently. This also allows us to recognise the true emotional need that underlies our reaction and again helps and supports us to find alternative ways of attending to this. If you don't know what is going on, how can you know to react differently?

Our attention is often described as the spotlight of our mind, and it is often the case that we naturally direct the spotlight of our attention externally (for example, toward situations around us, what other people are doing or experiencing etc.), and this means that we often miss a lot of important information about ourselves. I want to encourage you to gently turn the spotlight of your attention to observe and notice what is happening in your body, your thoughts and your emotions.

Mindful attention

One way of doing this is to get into a habit of taking your "emotional temperature" by regularly checking in and starting to notice what you are thinking and feeling.

First of all, gently direct your attention to yourself - try to simply observe what is there.

Sit in a comfortable position - upright with your feet planted on the floor. Now, bring your attention to any physical feelings (external, internal), any emotions that are there and any thoughts. At this point, all you have to do is notice them without trying to change them.

This initial step of checking in with yourself may be enough to practice for now. It is helpful if you can try to do this a few times a day to begin with. After a while, you might want to move on to the next part, which involves learning to slow down your emotional response.

Ways of building in a pause and calming your brain: slowing down

When we experience strong, intense emotions, these feelings tend to hijack our brain. This has been described as an amygdala hijack (Goleman, 2005). The amygdala is the part of our brain which is connected with primitive emotions, and when it is activated, it can be hard to access logical/rational thought (located in the frontal lobes of the brain). The body's fight-or-flight response is controlled by the sympathetic nervous system, which is one part of the autonomic nervous system. The other part is the parasympathetic nervous system, which works to relax and slow down the body's response.

The sympathetic nervous system is our "alarm" system, which is wired so efficiently that it acts incredibly quickly, to the extent that we don't even have time to consciously process what is happening (that's why people jump out of the path of an oncoming car before they fully process what is happening). Activation of the sympathetic nervous system triggers many automatic physical reactions to get us ready to fight or escape. These reactions include increased heart rate, breathing quickly, muscles tensing, pupils dilating and restlessness.

The parasympathetic system counteracts this system - it is known as the "rest and digest" system. Many of the strategies that follow in this chapter focus on bringing this system online to calm the nervous system (turning down the volume on the amygdala) so you can slow down and think more clearly. The parasympathetic system is associated with safety, relaxation and conservation of energy. To calm the mind, we need to calm the body. There is more information on this in Chapter 7 (Exit 4).

Here are some different options to try, or you could combine these.

1 Focus your attention on your body.

- Focus your attention on your breath - take slow, deep breaths - notice where the breath goes to - you may even want to place a hand on that part of your body. Imagine the breath as being like a gentle wave moving in and out of the shoreline. Keep this going for a few breaths and notice how your body starts to calm along with your mind.
- Another option is to hold your hands gently (not clasping) - notice the pressure, feel and weight of your hands. And with your feet, notice the full contact of the sole of your foot with the ground - apply gentle pressure to increase the sense of connection with the ground.

2   Ground yourself and reconnect to the present moment. When we are caught up in emotion, our minds tend to get caught up in thoughts, and our minds run away with us (usually towards past events or feared future events). Each one of these thoughts/feared scenarios triggers a new wave of emotion that keeps us emotionally activated. If we can reconnect to the present moment, we can anchor ourselves back in reality, and we can deal with things more effectively.

There are different ways of reconnecting to the present:

- Identify a particular smell that you associate with feeling safe or comforted – it might be a perfume, a hand cream or an essential oil. You could try putting some on a handkerchief so that you can carry it with you. Research shows that our sense of smell is very connected to the amygdala, so this can be a very fast and effective way of calming the mind.
- Focus on an aspect of your environment – 5, 4, 3, 2, 1 exercise.

---

5 – notice 5 things you can see
4 – notice 4 things you can feel
3 – notice 3 things you can hear
2 – notice 2 things you can smell
1 – notice 1 thing you can taste

The rationale behind these exercises is to calm your brain so that you can reorient to the present moment. These are important steps in helping you to slow your automatic reactions and build in a pause. It is similar to stopping for a break to check the map and reorient yourself when you are on a journey.

We will now move on to the following strategies that focus on helping you gain clarity and perspective.

Noticing and questioning your reaction

This involves looking at your thought processes and interpretations of triggering situations or events. As we discussed in Chapter 3, the way you view and interpret triggers strongly influences your emotional reaction, so therefore, it makes sense to stop, reflect and question these thought processes. The way we react is likely to be related to our past experiences, and this means that certain situations or events are more likely to be triggering (we all have our own personal "hot spots" because of our past experiences). This is why we sometimes have very strong and intense reactions to situations. However, if you are anything like me, you will also have had the experience where, once the heat has gone out of the situation, you will be left wondering why on earth you viewed the situation in that way and had such a strong reaction!

Our thought processes and self-talk reflect the way we interpret situations/events (triggers). I am referring to the private, internal conversation you have in your mind where you may comment, reflect and pass judgement on what is happening. It is this internal self-talk and these thought processes that drive our emotional reaction when we encounter a trigger. These interpretations and thought processes are unique to the individual, so the way one person interprets a situation will be different to how another person interprets it. These individual interpretations lead to people having different emotional reactions to exactly the same situation.

Trigger ───────▶ Interpretation & self-talk ───────▶ Emotional reaction

The problem is that these patterns of interpretations and thoughts become very automatic, fast and habitual, so we don't really notice or question them. They become like background noise, so we are tuned out of them even though they are still driving our emotional reactions and our behaviour. We need to turn the volume up on them so we can notice, pay attention and hear them. If we turn our attention towards our thoughts and emotions, we can become far more aware and question them.

It is important to be clear that I am not suggesting that some thoughts are "right" and others are "wrong" or that we just have to think positively all the time – that's not realistic and can be problematic in itself. The aim is to start thinking flexibly and finding a balanced perspective on the situation. We are trying to find alternative choices and exits earlier on in the emotional eating journey. Rather than just focusing on making changes

Thought Diary

Day/time	Situation or trigger	Emotions – what emotions did you feel?	Thoughts - What were you thinking about the situation? What were you saying to yourself?	Can you recognise a particular thinking pattern?			
Monday	Friend made upsetting comment about what I was wearing	Sadness, anger	I knew I looked stupid. Why did I even bother trying to make an effort? I will always be alone.	Judge/Bully Fortune telling			

Figure 4.3 Thought diary to track triggers, thoughts and interpretations of triggers and emotional responses

towards the end of the emotional eating route, we are focusing on making changes to the thoughts and emotions connected to the triggers.

Exploring your interpretations and reactions to triggers

To start the process of tuning in to your reactions and interpretations to triggers, it is helpful to keep a "thought diary". Don't worry, this doesn't mean that you need to write down every thought that enters your mind! We just want to focus on the interpretations and thoughts that are associated with significant changes in your emotions (which then impact eating). Most people find it easier to tune in to what they are feeling rather than what they are thinking at first, so you might want to use changes in your emotions as a prompt to complete this diary. So, for example, if you notice that you are feeling anxious, sad, stressed etc., that would be your prompt to start thinking about what happened before, i.e. what was the trigger? And then what were you thinking/saying to yourself about the trigger?

You can think of your emotions as being like the weather, so when there is a sudden change in your (emotional) temperature, that would be your prompt to tune into your emotions and notice what you are thinking or saying to yourself. The quotes that follow really show the benefits of being able to recognise and question the thought processes that arise in response to a trigger.

> *When I hit a trigger, I now recognise what is going on. I recognise the pattern. I go to eat . . . and now I stop and take 10 seconds and ask myself "why are you doing this . . . what is this telling you? . . . It is like being your own therapist. I say to myself "you want to eat X, but imagine how that is going to feel in your stomach afterwards . . . is that feeling something you want? What is the emotion . . . stress? procrastination? Is eating going to make that go away or is it going to be there afterwards?" There is a real power in asking yourself those questions.*
>
> *DJ*

> *Writing down and journaling helps - it gives me distance and helps me figure things out and why I am feeling that way at that particular time. For me, writing down my thoughts can really help with anxiety. You are allowing your brain to process the thoughts, rather than push them away.*
>
> *PM*

When you become more familiar with identifying the thoughts that occur in response to a trigger, then you might notice that there are certain patterns to these. It can be useful to categorise these by seeing if they fall into any of the patterns described in the table that follows - are there any patterns that you recognise? You might notice that there are a few different ones that apply to your thoughts. This process of recognising your interpretations and reactions can help you to start to step back, label them and gain some distance from them.

Recognising familiar thought patterns and interpretations

Thinking habit	Descriptions	Example
All or nothing	Thinking in extremes only - no in-between options (good/bad; success/failure)	If I don't get something 100% right, I've failed. If I slip up, then I've completely ruined things.
The Judge/Bully	Judging and being highly self-critical. Using negative labels and name-calling.	I am a failure. I am lazy.
Mental filter	Only paying attention to negative evidence that fits our beliefs. Ignoring positive or neutral info.	I always get things wrong. Here we go again . . . I knew I'd mess it up.
Catastrophising	Focusing on worst-case scenarios/focusing on small details and losing perspective.	This is a complete disaster. I'm going to lose my job, my home, my family.
Mind reading	Believing that we know what others are thinking	Everyone is looking and thinking "she looks a complete mess". My colleagues are noticing how much food I am eating and thinking "no wonder she is overweight".
Fortune telling	Making negative predictions about the future (without evidence) and believing the predictions.	I'll never get the job. I will never find a partner who will accept me. I will always be alone.

Managing your automatic interpretations and reactions

You may find it helpful to start asking yourself some of the following questions that will enable you to explore your immediate reactions and thought processes.

LABELLING AND QUESTIONING THE INTENSITY OF YOUR REACTION

- How would you label your automatic reaction? Is there a particular thinking habit that you can identify?
- How proportionate is your reaction to the situation?
- Does this reaction tap into a previous experience, or is it reactivating a memory?
- How likely are you to think about this situation or your reaction later in the day, tomorrow, next week?

SHIFTING PERSPECTIVE

Can you remember a time when you have supported a friend who is struggling with a problem? Most people find that it is easier to see things more clearly and identify other possibilities compared to if they are trying to do that for themselves. When we think about another person's problem, we tend to do this from a different perspective, which then provides clarity. The mental distance that we have from the friend's problem really helps us to be flexible and gain perspective. The following questions will help you to start shifting your own perspective on triggers that you may experience:

- How might someone else view the situation?
- What would be an alternative way of viewing the situation?
- What would you say to a friend in a similar situation?

ZOOMING OUT

When we are experiencing difficult or challenging emotions, we tend to lose perspective and get tangled up in details which makes it difficult to see the bigger picture. I know I have had many experiences of getting anxious or upset about things and then, after the event, wondered why on earth I got so worked up! Our minds tend to circle back to the things that we are upset about, which means that we pay more attention to them, and then they naturally take up more space in our minds. By zooming out and seeing the bigger picture, you can start to make choices and decisions because you can see things more clearly.

You could try taking a helicopter view of the situation - imagine that you are in a helicopter, hovering above the situation that is causing you distress. When a helicopter takes off and gets higher and higher, it is less involved with the small details at the ground level. The pilot has full vision of the terrain and landscape, not the tiny details. You could also use the analogy of standing on top of a mountain and looking down at the terrain. This process of mentally zooming out when you feel strong emotions can help to create mental distance and gain clarity.

Make an active decision about whether you can change the trigger

There are some triggers that are beyond our control (e.g. we can't control if our boss is in a bad mood or a friend forgets an important date), but there are others that we may be able to influence. It is worth making a very clear distinction so that you can try to either actively manage the trigger or accept that this is not possible in this situation and instead, focus on managing your response to the trigger.

To make this distinction, you must notice and pay attention to the trigger to make an active decision. You might want to ask yourself if there is anything that you can realistically do to address the issue. Are there other options?

If the answer is "yes", then the obvious option is to problem-solve and think about what steps you can take. To help with this, you could also think about what you might advise someone else in a similar situation to do.

If the answer is "no", and you are not able to do anything to change the actual trigger (i.e. it is not within your control), then your focus should shift to dealing with the consequences of the trigger and how you respond. The strategies outlined in the next few sections of the book will cover various options, including how to manage the emotions and thoughts that arise and alternatives to emotional eating behaviours.

Key points and tasks to work on

- Try to build a habit of learning to check in with yourself – notice how you are feeling physically and emotionally.
- You can learn to slow down and build in a pause after encountering a trigger.
- It is helpful to slow down and calm the body – bring yourself back to the present moment through breathing exercises.
- Notice and question your reaction – can you spot any particular thinking patterns in your interpretation of triggers? Start to label your thinking patterns, question your thoughts, shift perspective and zoom out so you can see the bigger picture.
- Make an active decision about whether you can do anything to change or address the trigger or if you need to focus on managing your reaction to the trigger.

Reference

Goleman, D. (2005). *Emotional intelligence: Why it can matter more than IQ*. Bantam Books.

Chapter 5
Exit 2
Understanding and managing emotions

This is the second exit from the automatic emotional eating route. In this chapter, we will focus on recognising and labelling emotions, decoding emotional signals and building your understanding of emotions (and your reactions to them). This is important because people often cope with emotions through avoiding or suppressing them, and this creates difficulties. In this chapter, you will update your understanding of emotions and start to experiment with making space for emotions and using them as a compass to guide your actions.

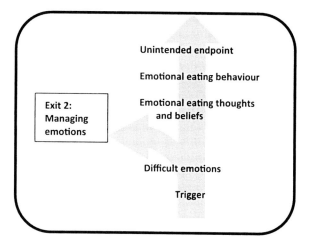

Understanding emotions - figuring out the meaning of specific emotions

In Chapter 3, we briefly started to identify the specific emotions connected with your emotional eating. In this next section, we will focus on learning to decode the signal or messages that underpin these emotions.

Emotions have an important evolutionary function because they signal something to us. Each emotion has a unique theme and meaning. Once you have figured out which emotions impact on your eating, it can then be helpful to identify the underlying meaning of the emotion because this is a clue about the motivation or unmet need. This can help you to consider more helpful ways of addressing this motivation or need other than through eating. The following list shows the underlying meaning or signal of some common emotions:

DOI: 10.4324/9781032664354-9

Emotion	Typical meaning of this emotion
Stress	I am overwhelmed and can't cope with all the demands.
Shame	My behaviour may lead to others rejecting or ostracising me.
Boredom	I need mental stimulation.
Anger	It's unfair and unjust.
Sadness	I feel the absence or loss of (person, connection, activity).
Anxiety	I feel threatened or in danger.
Guilt	I have done something wrong, caused harm or broken a rule.

You have already identified the most common emotions connected to emotional eating in Chapter 3. Make a note of them in the table that follows. If you now look at the examples of emotions and meanings listed earlier, do they correspond with your experiences? What is the meaning or signal associated with the common emotions which trigger your emotional eating? The underlying meaning might be similar to those listed earlier, but it might be worded slightly differently so feel free to adapt it accordingly.

Exercise

Which emotions are connected with eating?	What is the underlying signal or meaning of this emotion? What does it tell you? What message is the emotion communicating?

If you can identify the underlying need or message attached to an emotion and start to directly address it, then eating becomes a far less obvious part of the solution.

How do you usually respond to your emotions?

By this stage you should hopefully have started to recognise your emotions and the messages they are communicating, but what happens next? It is very common for people to invalidate, dismiss and discount their emotions or emotional reactions. You often hear people saying things like:

"I shouldn't be feeling upset".
"It's so silly to be anxious about this".
"Other people have much bigger problems".
"I'm pathetic for feeling this way".
"I know it's silly, but . . ."

The message underlying these responses is that you shouldn't be experiencing the emotion, and that the emotional reaction is not valid or justified. The emotion is then pushed aside and the message is ignored.

Why is this a problem?

- It means people don't pay attention or address their emotions.
- And then the emotions tend to simmer, increase and become more unpredictable.
- It creates an emotional chain reaction - for example, a person's anxiety may then lead to frustration, which leads to guilt and shame.
- And the person loses confidence in their ability to manage their emotions.
- And on top of that, the person doesn't address the initial problem or issue triggering the emotional reaction!

The quote that follows clearly shows the impact of being in a family environment where emotions were not validated or acknowledged.

I don't know if my parents were very emotionally aware . . . . so when I displayed emotions, they didn't respond well . . . I was expected to be "good" and any sort of emotional turmoil would not be met with sympathy. It would be met with a logical response like, "you can't be upset about this because of x, y and z" and whilst those were the facts, I often felt that they didn't understand why I was upset so I would turn to something else for comfort. I knew that a lot of my thoughts and emotions were not logical but then I just felt bad about them . . . which then resulted in me finding something else that would make me feel better and eating always did that. It took away the feeling of being ashamed or silly for feeling whatever feeling I was experiencing, and I would then focus on something else (eating). Once that was over, I knew I could focus on feeling bad about what I had eaten rather than feeling the emotions so eating became a diversion strategy.

PFM

We may wish that we hadn't experienced a particular emotion, but we don't choose to have emotions - our bodies and brains are designed to experience emotion. As you can see from the quote that follows, it is important to acknowledge emotions because they are a normal and natural part of our existence. It is the response to the emotion that really matters.

I now know that emotions are telling me something. They are part of who we are. I am not abnormal to have these emotions, they are part of being human. They are not necessarily a bad thing. I've always focused on the extreme emotions - the terrible or amazing - so I have bounced between the two extremes. However, that means I am not living in the reality of life because we experience a whole range of emotions, good and bad, as part of our everyday life and these change hour by hour. I now realise there is much more variation in my emotions and that I am in the middle ground more than I realised.

BJ

The process of starting to acknowledge and respect emotional signals means turning towards and paying attention to emotions whilst allowing them to be there - not trying to push them away or get rid of them. Sometimes, people misinterpret this encouragement to tune into their emotions as meaning that they have to fully immerse themselves in really painful, difficult emotions making it a really extreme full-on experience, almost like a white-knuckle ride! Thankfully, this is not the aim or intention behind these ideas. It is about gently noticing and creating space for what is already there. It also means not making judgements about emotions and the validity of them. If you ignore or push away your emotions, then it is difficult to figure out what is happening and what you might need. It is also a way of building up confidence in your ability and stamina to manage emotions.

Exercise

If someone you knew and cared deeply about was distressed, would you:

ignore them?

tell them to stop being ridiculous?

that they "shouldn't" be feeling distressed?

What would you do? (circle any that you recognise and add any others)

- Listen to them
- Try to make sense of their feelings (e.g. "I can see why the disagreement with your boss would make you feel upset and angry".
- Empathise
- Let them know that you will support them
- Any others . . . ?

And how do you think your friend would feel in response to your input?

- What would happen to the intensity of their emotions?

What has this got to do with eating?

If you learn to develop skills in noticing and making space for emotions (even challenging ones), this will, over time, reduce your dependency on food as a way of coping with these feelings.

Beliefs about emotions

The way we are raised and the early messages that we are given about emotions really impact how we respond to them later in life, as you can see:

> *I grew up believing that negative emotions are basically bad – in my family, you weren't allowed to express them. A lot of effort went into masking my emotions. It was best to keep your mouth shut so I pretended to be happy all the time because that was safer.*
>
> BJ

How do you view your own emotions?

Often, people want to get "rid" of difficult or challenging emotions that might feel uncomfortable. Understandably, they simply don't want to have to feel those difficult emotions. However, the strategies that people use to get rid of or control their emotions often tend to backfire and create a bigger and/or different problem. It is very common for people to eat as a mechanism to avoid or suppress thoughts and feelings (as you can see in the quotes that follow). This is often driven by an underlying fear of emotions. On one level, it makes sense to avoid emotions if you find them deeply uncomfortable and are worried about how to cope with them.

Eating was a way of numbing or not thinking about my feelings. It was also an emotional reset . . . so once I was eating the food it was almost like closing the door on the emotion and it was my way of coping.

DK

I eat to shut down my emotions. I worry that if I don't eat, then they will increase and then I might upset or offend people around me because I will behave in a way that is out of character. I eat in order to control this.

ZG

Fear of emotions inevitably leads to working hard to avoid these feelings. It's a bit like if someone is fearful of dogs, then they generally go out of their way to avoid contact with them, but this means they rely on avoidance as a coping strategy. It also means that they never gather evidence or confidence that they can be around dogs without something bad happening. It's the same with emotions – fear of emotions leads to avoidance of emotions, which, in turn, reduces confidence in the ability to manage them in future and over-reliance on eating as a way of coping with them.

Exercise

Let's take some time to consider how you react to your emotions. Start by thinking about some of the most common emotions which impact your eating. Now choose one of these emotions (e.g. stress, anxiety, sadness) and try to bring to mind a recent time when you experienced this emotion – try to picture where you were, what was happening etc.

When you experienced this emotion, how did you respond to the emotion? What was your reaction to it? How much discomfort did it create (rate on a scale of 1–10, 10 = maximum discomfort)?

Did you notice a desire to move away from the emotion or to "get rid" of it?

Was there anything that you did to avoid the emotion?

Is there any "cost" attached to avoiding the emotion?

Updating your understanding about emotions

In Chapter 2, we discussed the idea that the strategies that we use to manage our emotions may have been helpful in the distant past (e.g. as a means to suppress or avoid emotions) but are no longer serving us well. This next section provides an opportunity to update your understanding of emotions as a first step towards increasing your openness and acceptance of them.

There are no "bad" emotions

There are some important lessons about emotions that we are often not taught as we grow up. Some of the typical messages that we may have received are that negative or challenging emotions are "wrong" and that if we don't get rid of them, then they will increase in intensity and that we should just "get on" (doing mode) rather than noticing and responding to our emotions. This is one of the reasons why people tend to react to their emotions by eating, because they believe this is a way of reducing the feeling. The quotes that follow show the problems that this fear and avoidance of emotions can lead to:

> *There was a fear of experiencing my emotions and I avoided wanting to feel anything negative so I used food as that escape. I would recognise the warning signs of those feelings coming and I used food as the escape. When I was eating the food, it stopped me from thinking about the feelings. Food was a barrier that I put up as a way of protecting myself . . . but longer term it actually created more of an issue by not addressing the feelings but also contributed to the eating and weight issues too.*
>
> DK

> *Emotions are really strong and they can control me. I can get lost in them. They can consume me. It feels like a battle sometimes. I can use the food to control my moods. If I feel overwhelmed, I can use food as a way to cut off and feel numb.*
>
> BJ

The problem with eating as a coping mechanism to control or suppress emotions is that the person never gets to find out that the emotion would naturally change regardless of whether they eat.

Our emotions are always changing . . . and so does their intensity

Just for a second, imagine that you allowed the feeling of . . . (anxiety/sadness/stress etc.) to remain as it is, without actively doing anything to "get rid of it". What do you imagine would happen to the feeling? Do you anticipate it would increase? decrease? Change into another feeling?

Emotions change in intensity moment by moment. People sometimes worry that they will be "trapped" in their negative feelings and that unless they "do" something to get rid of these emotions, they will continue to feel distressed or uncomfortable. However, if we flip this round the other way, then we don't tend to have the same beliefs about "positive" emotions like happiness, excitement etc. – we never think we will be trapped in happiness forever, so why would it be any different for anxiety, sadness or the other emotions we dislike?

These concerns about being trapped in negative emotions means that people often take steps to try to control or get rid of their emotions, as you can see:

> *I am triggered when I am confronted with a problem or negative feedback or something that requires action on my part . . . and then I don't know what to do and I worry about making the wrong decision. I become overwhelmed with having to make a decision, and the pressure of doing it correctly. Instead of taking a moment to slow down and think it through, the first thing that happens is I want to get up from my desk and go to get something to eat because then I don't have to deal with it . . . eating creates a gap for me and I can take a break from the problem. In my mind I think the food has helped me calm down and figure out what to do next, but in reality, it is just taking some time away from the problem. I could step away and pretty much do anything else . . . I could work on something else, close my emails etc. . . . but my learned response is just to go and eat something.*
>
> PFM

This person recognises their belief that "food helps me calm down" is an inaccurate belief and that in reality, it is taking time out which makes the difference.

Imagine that someone views stress as an unpleasant, aversive emotion that they cannot tolerate, and so they eat. As their stress levels start to come down, they attribute this reduction in their stress to the act of eating. In future, this connection that "eating reduces stress" then starts to influence their future decision to eat in response to stress. The pathway is set in the brain. As a result of this belief, the person never gets to find out that the feeling of stress would naturally change anyway (like all emotions). In this scenario, eating is similar to putting on a sticking plaster on when none is actually required.

The other problem is that because our brains are so good at learning, the emotional eating reaction starts to get triggered much earlier. Our brain becomes the equivalent of a hypervigilant security guard that is waiting for the first sign of (emotional) trouble before stepping in or a personal surveillance system which scans for danger and gets triggered very easily. As the behaviour gets triggered earlier and faster, it becomes almost like an automatic reflex. Imagine that originally, someone might have needed to reach a very intense level of anxiety (e.g. a 9 out of 10) before it triggered eating. Over time, this is likely to have reduced so that the intensity of the emotion may only need to reach a 4/10 to trigger the same eating response.

So rather than viewing emotions as static, it helps to view emotions as fluctuating and flowing. Emotions naturally change and move, and if you allow them to be there and give them space, they will naturally flow and shift. The extra effort that we put into controlling emotions means they have limited space to move and therefore they get stuck. This is why it is important to create space for emotions even if they are associated with discomfort. I know this can be a difficult or even counterintuitive step to take, but the idea is to welcome all emotions and remember that they are trying to signal something to you. The aim is to learn to build up your willingness to experience and tolerate all emotions. Why? Because, as you can see from the quote that follows, by doing this you will find that emotions naturally shift, and you aren't putting an extra layer of struggle or control on top which then means you rely on eating.

I have always felt that I have to do something to deal with emotions and I didn't like the idea - it feels con-frontational and terrifying. When we did the exercise of making space for emotions, it was refreshing to realise that it is ok to experience emotions and you don't have to do anything with them - you can observe them and let them be there. I've been practicing making space for emotions and it has helped me to see that these things change, they are not permanent. Although I know logically that emotions are not permanent, it can feel very overwhelming in that moment and it feels like you have to do something with it but often you don't . . . you can just pause and make space and let it pass.

PFM

 Exercise

- Just try an experiment - notice what you are feeling now. How would you describe the emotion or combination of emotions? How intense are the emotions on a scale of 1-10 (10 = most extreme)?

- Now check your watch or clock and note down what time it is.

- Then set an alarm for 3 minutes.

- How would you label the emotion or combination of emotions you are feeling now? How intense are the emotions on a scale of 1-10?

- Recheck in another 3 minutes.

- How would you label the emotion or combination of emotions you are feeling now? How would you rate the intensity now?

- What happened to your emotions over this time period?

You can allow emotions to remain

How do you stop avoiding emotions and make space for them? The following approach was developed by Russ Harris (2022), and it is from a type of therapy called Acceptance and Commitment Therapy (ACT).

Try to bring to mind a recent time when you experienced one of the emotions that is associated with emotional eating. You might recall the last time you felt stressed or angry or anxious. Then, when you have brought that situation into your mind's eye and you can connect with the emotion, I want you to work through the following steps:

- **Observe** – notice where you are feeling the emotion in your body – your chest, stomach, neck, shoulders, hands. Can you visualise the emotion? Is it a certain shape or colour? Temperature?
- **Breathe** – as you observe the feeling, breathe into it. Imagine the breath flowing into and around the feeling.
- **Expand** – as you breathe into it, imagine space opening inside you . . . open up around the feeling and create space for it. You are bigger than the feeling.
- **Allow** – allow the feeling to be there. You don't have to like it or want it, just allow it. Changing the feeling or getting rid of it is not the goal. Your goal is simply to let it be. The feeling is still there, but it is only part of you.

How do you feel at the end of the exercise? What has happened to the emotion?

You can listen to emotions and use them as a compass to guide your actions

We have now considered how to validate and make space for emotions, but we also want to consider how you might want to use the emotional signal to guide your decisions and actions. There are different ways in which you can use these "emotional signals":

1   To identify and address any unmet needs – what are the emotions telling you that you actually need? If you listen to the meaning of the emotion, what are you missing or what do you need?

2   To help you to guide your choices and decisions to do the things that truly matter to you. This means being prepared to experience a degree of emotional discomfort because your goals and values matter more to you. In order to tolerate discomfort, there has to be a good reason that is more powerful and important than the discomfort. For example, going to a friend's birthday party may make you feel anxious, and you might have thoughts about wanting to stay in and avoid the situation. Or you could make the choice to go despite being anxious, because the values you hold about being a supportive friend and feeling connected with others matter more. Part of this involves being clear about what truly matters to you as an individual and the type of person you want to be. Here are some questions that you can ask yourself to identify your values – for example, Who do I want to be? What's important to me? What qualities do I want to display? At the end of my life, how do I want to be described as a person? You can then consider how you can use the answers to these questions to guide your choices and behaviour in the present moment, when you may be experiencing challenging emotions.

3   You can use the emotional signal to help cue you to respond differently or make a different choice – something which may meet your needs more effectively or, at the very least, let you experience less psychological distress after the event. So, for example, if you are feeling anxious because of your workload and notice that you are procrastinating (and eating may play a role in this), then an alternative approach would be to break the tasks down and engage with them rather than avoid.

You might want to spend some time considering and planning how you want to respond to your emotional signals in future. What choices can you make in future based on your common emotional signals? What do you want and need? How can these emotions guide you like a compass to do what is important to you?

Key points and tasks to work on

- Update your understanding of emotions - they flow, move and fluctuate.
- Notice your reactions to emotions as they arise - notice the temptation to "get rid of" them or push them away.
- Practice creating space for emotions.
- Acknowledge that you are prepared to experience emotional discomfort to make a choice to focus on what truly matters to you. Let the emotional signal act as a compass to guide your behaviour.

Reference

Harris, R. (2022). *The Happiness Trap*. Robinson.

Chapter 6
Exit 3

Managing and updating the emotional eating thought ladder

This is our third exit from the familiar emotional eating route. We will focus on identifying and learning to manage the different types of thoughts and beliefs on the emotional eating thought ladder. The chapter is divided into two sections. In Part 1 of this chapter, we will identify different types of emotional eating thoughts – "want" thoughts, decision-based thoughts and underlying emotional eating beliefs. In Part 2, you will learn strategies to help you manage and respond to your emotional eating thoughts. You will develop strategies to create distance between you and some of your emotional eating thoughts as well as questioning and updating your emotional eating beliefs.

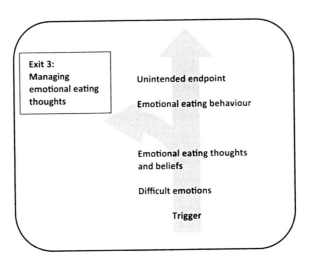

Figure 6.1 Exit 3: Managing emotional eating thoughts

Part 1

Identifying the different types of thoughts on the emotional eating ladder

In Chapter 3, we discussed how connections between emotions and eating develop. Certain emotions are likely to activate thoughts about food and decisions about eating. These emotional eating thoughts act as a bridge between the emotion and emotional eating behaviour.

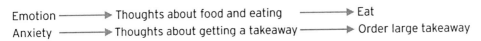

Take a moment to consider the fact that not everyone makes the decision to eat in response to stress or sadness. This means that there must be a thought process that somehow bridges the gap between the emotion and eating. If we can focus on identifying your specific emotional eating thoughts and learn how to manage and respond to them differently, then there is no longer a direct bridge to emotional eating!

DOI: 10.4324/9781032664354-10

In Chapter 3, I briefly introduced you to the concept of the emotional eating thought ladder. Just to recap, the idea is that there are different levels and rungs of emotional eating thoughts and beliefs that influence emotional eating. We only tend to be conscious of the noisy, intrusive food thoughts at the top of the ladder, but there are other emotional eating thought processes underneath that drive these. In this chapter, we are going to identify the different types of emotional eating thoughts, starting from the top of the ladder and working down to the deeper thoughts (beliefs). By doing this, you can then learn the skills to manage and update these thoughts so they have less impact. We are going to work through each rung on the emotional eating ladder so that you can identify your thoughts and the connections between them. Note that you can climb either up or down the ladder – the underlying beliefs about emotional eating drive the surface-level food thoughts (from bottom up), but also, the surface-level food thoughts tap into the underlying emotional eating beliefs (top down).

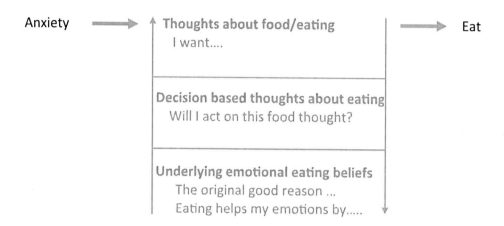

Figure 6.2 Different types of thoughts on the emotional eating ladder

What does an emotional eating ladder look like?

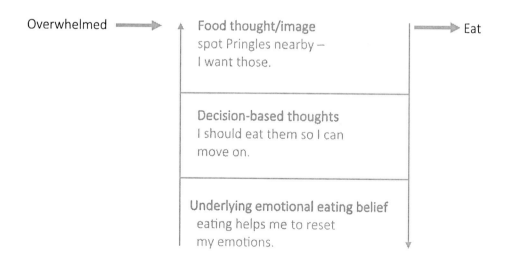

Figure 6.3 Example of an emotional eating thought ladder

We may only notice the initial food-related thought or image ("I want those"), but this thought is underpinned by deeper beliefs that connect food and mood. When we connect these thoughts, they reveal a meaningful and logical thought process that explains the reason for eating and, subsequently, the person's decision to eat. This is why simply challenging the "surface-level" food thoughts (i.e. by saying "I don't need that") can often be futile and ineffective, because it fails to take into account and address the underlying emotional eating beliefs. These

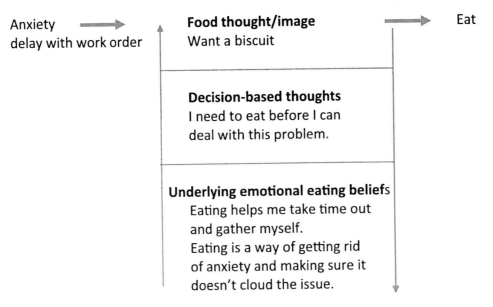

Figure 6.4 Example of an emotional eating thought ladder

linked thoughts create a meaningful "emotional eating story", which is shown based on the following example of an emotional eating ladder.

My emotional eating story: When I feel anxious, I have thoughts about wanting certain foods (biscuits in this scenario). I decide to act on these food thoughts before I deal with the problem. The reason for this is that eating gives me time out and helps push the anxiety aside so it doesn't get in the way.

The idea is that by becoming more aware of our "hidden" thought processes and looking at the connections between them, we can make sense of the behaviour but also start to update and manage these thoughts differently.

Climbing the emotional eating thought ladder – which food thoughts and choices do you recognise?

We are going to work through the different types of emotional eating thoughts you may encounter on the ladder.

The thoughts on the top rung of the emotional eating ladder – the "want" thoughts

When you experience a trigger, the first emotional eating urge that you might notice is intrusive thoughts (or images) about food which preoccupy your mind. People often tend to have particular foods or types of food that they crave in response to specific emotions, e.g. a takeaway, specific snacks or nostalgic foods. These thoughts tend to have a particular quality and tone to them – they are noisy, intrusive, loud, dominating. It is more likely that you will notice thoughts about wanting specific foods rather than connected thoughts like "I'm feeling sad so I want chocolate" or "I am anxious and therefore I want a takeaway". You might notice that these thoughts begin . . .

- I want . . .
- I need . . .
- I fancy . . .
- I'll just . . .
- I must have . . .

In addition to these thoughts, you might have images or pictures of foods or meals that appear in your mind.

When you are experiencing the emotions which often lead to eating, what are your typical top-rung "want" food thoughts?

1

2

3

The thoughts on the middle rung of the emotional eating ladder – decision-based thoughts

The next set of emotional eating thoughts, the ones on the middle rung of the ladder, are those which involve making the decision to eat. They are usually a response to the initial intrusive thoughts about particular foods and involve making a decision about whether to act on these thoughts (these are often the "go on, do it" thoughts!). For example, someone might have a top-rung food thought such as "I want ice cream", which then leads to middle-rung decision-based thoughts of "I won't be able to stop thinking about it until I have it, so I might as well eat it". Following is a description of how challenging it can be to experience and manage the internal battle that arises from these thoughts.

> *Eating brings me a calmness. It quietens down my mind. It allows me to be numb. It gives me a stillness and numbness that I struggle to find myself. I'm usually very anxious before I eat and that manifests itself as arguments in my head about going to the shops to buy chocolate biscuits and it feels like a fight. And then the fight becomes too much so I then decide to eat. All the arguments about not going to the shop are peeled away and I am single-minded about going to the shop. I'm not eating for enjoyment or fulfilment, there's just a sense of relief that I am having a break from those thoughts and emotions.*
>
> *BJ*

These thoughts on the "middle rung" of the emotional eating ladder usually involve justifying, rationalising or giving oneself permission to act on the thoughts to eat. In that moment, the advantages of eating outweigh the disadvantages, and these thoughts are usually a way of creating the rationale to go ahead and eat.

We can categorise these type of decision-based thoughts. Are there any on the list that you recognise?

Permission giving	"I deserve a treat". "I need a reward". "I will start the plan again on Monday". "I've messed up".
Insistent/cravings/powerless to resist	"I want/need chocolate . . . I might as well have it otherwise I won't get the thoughts of chocolate out of my head". "I need to get this out of my system".
Defiance/expression	"Blow it . . . I'm going to do what I want". "I want X so I'm going to have it".
Abandon/defeat	"I've broken the plan, so I might as well carry on and start again on Monday . . ." "I've got to get this out of my system now". "I have so much weight to lose, having X won't make any difference".

What are your typical middle-rung thoughts? Do they fall into a particular category?

1

2

3

Thoughts on the bottom rung of the emotional eating ladder – the original "good reason" and underlying emotional eating beliefs

The thoughts (beliefs) at the bottom of the emotional eating ladder are the deepest food and mood connections, which are often out of our awareness until we start exploring them. They are very important because they provide the ultimate reason and explanation for emotional eating and drive the behaviour. In Chapter 2, we started to consider how we constructed and learned the emotional eating route. These old associations and connections between food and mood are usually at the bottom of the emotional eating ladder. They drive the emotional eating pattern because they are the fundamental beliefs that formed about how emotional eating serves a purpose (remember, there is always an original motive and "good reason" for this behaviour). Figuring out the original "good reason" or beliefs driving the emotional eating can help us to identify what we are missing or the problem that we are trying to fix. If you look at the example that follows, in which HJ was triggered to eat after getting angry and frustrated with her family, it makes total sense to eat in the context of the underlying beliefs and thought processes.

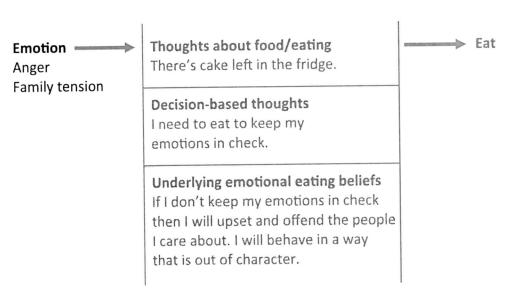

Figure 6.5 Example of an emotional eating ladder

The table that follows shows some typical examples of mood and food associations and emotional eating beliefs which are at the bottom of the emotional eating ladder. The list outlines some of the common associations and beliefs that people may have developed about how emotional eating helps in the short term. It takes time and patience to uncover these beliefs. These beliefs can be categorised to reflect different functions. Which do you recognise? Are there others that you need to add? Do any of these fit on your emotional eating ladder?

Emotional comfort or mood top-up	"Food makes me feel better". "Food provides pleasure". "Eating is a comfort when other things feel difficult".
Punishment/self-harm	"I deserve to feel bad". "I feel that I have done something bad/wrong, and I deserve to feel worse because of this".
Keep emotions at bay	"I can't let others see my emotions, and eating is a way of keeping them at bay so I can maintain my composure".
Distraction/respite	"Food stops me thinking". "The sensation of eating gives me something else to focus on rather than the thoughts". "Eating means I can avoid thinking about something".
Sabotage/self-fulfilling prophecy	"I have no control or willpower, and by eating, I prove this to myself".
Any others?	

What are your typical bottom-rung emotional eating beliefs? Do they fall into a particular category?

1

2

3

This next exercise is designed to help you recognise your thought processes on the different rungs of the emotional eating ladder.

Exercise – working down your emotional eating thought ladder Think back to the last time you ate in a way you were unhappy with... Rewind in your mind...Where were you? What was going on around you?	Trigger
Now try to recall the specific emotion that you were feeling ... (you might want to look back at the feelings wheel or list of emotions on p to help you narrow it down).	Which emotion did you experience?
Top rung – Now try to bring to mind the thoughts you had about food/eating ... Were there specific foods you were thinking about?	
Middle rung – And now, try to think about the decision that you made based on those initial food thoughts – how did you get from having those thoughts about the specific food item/type to making the decision to eat? How did you justify the decision to yourself? What was your rationale?	
Bottom rung – In that moment, how did you feel that eating would help your emotions? What would it give you? What would it take away?	

Figure 6.6 Mapping out your emotional eating thought ladder

Now, try to connect the thoughts so that you can see how the thoughts influence each other and create a logical story. Once you have created this summary, you might want to write this on a card or have it on your phone to refer to so that you can recognise when this "story" is happening.

Your emotional eating story

When I feel X . . . I have thoughts about wanting . . .
I then decide to act on these thoughts because . . .
The reason for this is . . .

It may take some time for you to work through the steps outlined above, so there is no need to rush on to Part 2 until you are ready.

Part 2

How can we learn to manage emotional eating thoughts differently?

The first thing to point out is that you have already done a lot of the hard work by noticing, labelling and mapping out your emotional eating thoughts on the ladder. This increased level of awareness often creates a degree of change automatically, so you have already taken a big step.

However, there are some additional steps that will help you learn how to manage these thoughts. I am going to introduce you to some different strategies that are helpful for dealing with the types of thoughts and beliefs that crop up on the different rungs on the emotional eating ladder. For the top-rung thoughts (the "want food" thoughts), learning how to notice and observe your thoughts from a distance (defusion) is helpful. Alongside this, learning to question and update the thoughts on the middle and bottom rungs of the emotional eating ladder helps to create long-lasting change. The idea is that if you can start to update and question the underlying beliefs and connections, then when the intrusive "want" thoughts about eating arise, you can step back from them. Just in case you are keen to know about the origins of these approaches, the strategies of questioning and updating thoughts derive from Cognitive-Behavioural Therapy (CBT) approach, whereas the strategy of defusion comes from Acceptance and Commitment Therapy (ACT). This will make sense as we work through it!

How to manage top-rung thoughts: developing skills in defusion

Just stop for a second and try to estimate how many thoughts per day you have.

It must be thousands and thousands! The question is, do you act on each of these thoughts, and if not, why not?

Our brains can figure out which thoughts to let pass by and which we need to act on in many areas of our life, but it is often much trickier to do this when it comes to food, especially when emotion is involved. The important thing to recognise is that we don't always fully engage or respond to our thoughts (thank goodness!). We can make decisions about whether our thoughts are helpful, are important and serve us well. In effect, our thoughts are just part of us, and ultimately, we can step back and make choices about how to react to them. You can't stop yourself from thinking, but you can choose how much attention you pay to your thoughts. So this next approach to managing thoughts involves learning to form a different relationship with our thoughts. It involves learning to notice and step back from our thoughts without getting tangled up in the content of them (either arguing with them about whether they are right/wrong or positive/negative) or feeling like we must obey them.

We sometimes have "sticky" thoughts that get stuck in our minds and then drive our behaviour - our minds can get hooked and tangled up in these thoughts, so we pay more attention to them, and they get bigger and louder until it is hard to think about anything else (we lose perspective and touch with reality). When it comes to thoughts about food, people often experience these as being intrusive and demanding. These thoughts can feel like instructions that we have to obey - like our brain is telling us we must act on the thought to eat a particular food. It can be liberating to realise that you don't have to do what your mind tells you to do - you can make a choice over how you respond. You can learn skills to "unhook" and disentangle yourself from these thoughts. Instead of fusing with your thoughts, you can learn to defuse from them so that you can notice and observe your thinking. I think of this as watching your thoughts rather than being "in" your thoughts. Why is this helpful? You can start to notice what your mind is telling you and then decide whether those thoughts work for you and whether they help you get closer to doing what truly matters to you.

So how do you do this? There are different ways that you can learn to create distance and defuse from your thoughts. The following strategies are based on ACT and come from the work of Russ Harris (2022). They build on the idea that our thoughts are separate from "us" and that we can create distance by viewing them as images or describing them in a different way. It is a way of externalising our thoughts. These may seem like odd and abstract ideas (they did to me at first!) but try to keep an open mind and give them a go.

IMAGE STRATEGIES

There are various images that you can use to picture your thoughts moving whilst "you" remain static observing your thoughts (this is similar to the idea that I discussed previously about your "noticing" mind being able to observe other mental processes). Most of these images involve some sort of movement, and this reflects the fact that thoughts change and move; they don't remain static in our minds.

You might want to just take a few moments and experiment with viewing your thoughts as words appearing in your mind. You could imagine them as appearing in a speech bubble or as words going across a screen. Are they moving? At what speed? What size are they? Can you just step back and notice them?

You can also try imagining that your thoughts come and go like leaves on a stream.

- Imagine that you are standing by a stream that is gently flowing along. Imagine how the ground feels beneath you, the sound of the water and the appearance of the water moving. Each time you notice a thought, feeling or sensation, imagine placing it on a leaf and letting it float down the stream. If your thoughts stop, just watch the stream. Sooner or later, your thoughts should start up again. Allow the stream to flow at its own rate. And when you are done, just bring your attention back to where you are.

You can try other options like:

- Imagining your thoughts coming and going like clouds in the sky
  Imagine that "you" are the sky, which is a permanent backdrop, it is always present behind the clouds. Imagine that your thoughts pass across and in front of the sky, like clouds moving.
- Imagining your thoughts coming and going like cars passing by
  Imagine standing at the side of a busy road and you are watching the cars come and go. Now imagine your thoughts to be like the cars that pass by - you can notice them without engaging.

Try these strategies with some of the thoughts you experience about particular foods - what happens if you step back, notice them and just let them pass by?

VERBAL STRATEGIES

Some people find it easier to use verbal strategies to help them step back from their thoughts. This approach helps to clarify that noisy food thoughts are just thoughts and cravings, not instructions which compel action. This reflects the idea that our thoughts are only part of us (ultimately, we are the boss!). There are some relatively simple but effective strategies you can use - so, for example, just think about the difference between saying to yourself:

"I want chocolate" compared to "I'm having the thought that I want chocolate".
"I want chocolate" compared to "My mind is telling me I want chocolate".
"I want chocolate" compared to "I notice that my mind is focusing on wanting chocolate".

When you test out the difference between the two thoughts, what do you notice about your emotional reaction? The noisiness of the thought? What might you do in response to the thought? How tempted might you be to get up and get the chocolate?

Now try this on some of your common thoughts from the emotional eating thought ladder. Try and notice how it sounds to express these thoughts slightly differently. What difference does it make?

Food thoughts – write down some of the common "want" thoughts that crop up for you.	Defusion techniques – which verbal or visual strategy will you try? How does it work?

How to manage middle-rung thoughts: challenging thoughts

The decision-based thoughts on the middle rung of the emotional eating ladder focus on deciding whether to go ahead and eat after having thoughts about specific foods (the top-rung thoughts). It is helpful to question and challenge these automatic decision-making thoughts so that they have less power and influence over your behaviour. Some of the ways that you can start to question and challenge these pesky thoughts include:

- What type or category of decision-based thought is this? Check the table on p. 61 to see if you can identify them. Label the thought process. For example, "these thoughts are permission-giving thoughts". This creates distance but also more accurately represents the psychological function of the thoughts, i.e. to give permission and to rationalise the decision.
- Other useful questions to ask include:
  - If I let this thought dictate my actions, where does this take me? When I buy into this thought or give it my full attention, how does my behaviour change?
  - How well do these decision thoughts serve me? Do they help me get closer to what I want? What evidence is there that this thought is helpful?
  - Based on my experience to date, would this be a good/wise decision in this situation? How will I feel about it in 20 minutes? Tomorrow?
  - What might I say to a friend who was having similar thoughts?

Use this table to identify some of your common decision-based thoughts and test out generating some alternative responses.

Decision thoughts	Alternatives
Example I deserve a treat. (permission giving)	If I act on this thought . . . I might feel better temporarily but then feel terrible. I've got used to treating myself with food, but there are other ways of treating myself.
I won't be able to get the food thoughts out of my head until I've eaten. (respite from thoughts)	It might be uncomfortable to experience these thoughts without eating, but that doesn't mean they will remain forever. I can refocus on other things. I can notice the thoughts and not act on them.

This approach focuses on unpicking the content of your thoughts and challenging them, but the alternative approach of defusion can also be used with these thoughts too. For example, you can notice that your mind is getting tangled with decision-based eating and name the category of thoughts, i.e. "here are my permission-giving thoughts".

How to manage bottom-rung thoughts: updating emotional eating thoughts and beliefs.

The thought processes at the bottom of the emotional eating ladder are rooted in well-worn pathways and tap into beliefs about the emotional function of eating, i.e. to lift mood, to be a treat, to reward, to numb or to shut down. As we discussed earlier, we often just blindly behave in accordance with these beliefs rather than investigate and question whether they serve the purpose that they once did. In Chapter 2, I referred to emotional eating patterns as an early or primitive attempt at problem-solving but one that has usually outlived its usefulness and effectiveness. In this next section, we are going to focus on questioning and updating these underlying emotional eating thoughts and beliefs, look at how effective they are and whether they serve us well in the present day.

Here are some questions which can be useful tools to facilitate updating your beliefs:

- What was the original good reason, motive or function for emotional eating?

- And how effectively does this work for you now? For how long? What are the positives that you get from it? And what are the costs of emotional eating?

- What is the mechanism whereby eating helps emotionally? And is this a reality or a belief? Bear in mind that there is a difference between something actually working versus believing that something works (a bit like a placebo pill).

- What might I say to a friend who was experiencing similar thoughts?

- What other ways are there for me to address the underlying need?

In the table that follows, try to write down your "old" emotional eating beliefs, and then try to update them using your responses to the questions. This process will help raise your awareness and prepare you for the next time these "old" beliefs get triggered.

Old beliefs	Updated beliefs
Example I need a food treat to look forward at the end of the day. Eating helps me get through. It lifts my mood.	Over the years, I have learned to associate eating as a treat and a way of managing stress. In reality, it only works temporarily and then tends to make me feel worse. The day is going to be difficult anyway. Food doesn't make a difference to that; it just tends to add to the problems.
Food helps me black out the other problems in my life. Eating gives me pleasure.	I learnt that eating junk food when I feel anxious or isolated makes me feel better. It gives me some short-term enjoyment. The reason it helps me black out from other things is that it takes my focus away and provides distraction. If food provides distraction and pleasure in the short term, then I can focus on finding other ways of meeting these needs. I can also think about if there is anything I can do to address the actual problems that are concerning me.

You can also use defusion as a strategy with these emotional eating beliefs. You can step back and recognise the familiar "story" that you tell yourself about how food is a treat or reward.

It is easy for people to inadvertently slip into being self-critical and judgemental about their emotional eating patterns, but it is important to remember that there was a "good reason" originally and to show compassion and understanding for yourself. Most people inherently know that emotional eating doesn't "work" for them but still find it difficult to stop the pattern because of their old food and mood associations and connections. In order to break these associations, we have to gather evidence that responding differently – not continuing to follow the familiar emotional eating route – is manageable and doesn't lead to negative consequences. I could spend a lot of time trying to convince you about this, but ultimately, you need to gather your own evidence and test it out yourself. I want you to pay attention to what happens if you respond differently to your thoughts – either by defusing from them, challenging them or updating them. If you do not blindly act in accordance with your thoughts, what happens? What difference does it make to your behaviour? How do you feel? What are the advantages and disadvantages?

Key points and tasks to work on

- Identify the thoughts on your emotional eating ladder – your top-rung "want" thoughts, the middle-rung decision-based thoughts and the emotional eating beliefs of the bottom rung.
- Recognise the type/category of these thoughts and label them.
- Experiment with defusion techniques to create distance between you and your thoughts.
- Challenge your decision-based thoughts.
- Update your emotional eating beliefs.
- Notice the impact of responding differently to thoughts – what are the consequences?

Reference

Harris, R. (2022). *The Happiness Trap*. Robinson.

Chapter 7
Exit 4

Developing alternative behaviours –
short-term and longer-term options to look after
your mind and body

This is our fourth exit from the familiar emotional eating route. This is the last of the possible exit routes I am going to focus on in this workbook, and this chapter has been written in collaboration with Dr Esme Banting, Clinical Psychologist. The chapter focuses on different behaviours that you can implement as an alternative to emotional eating. In Part 1, we will focus on strategies that you can use whilst you are experiencing the urge to emotionally eat. In Part 2, we will move on to building some longer-term "behavioural foundations" which will help you develop supportive ways of caring for yourself emotionally and physically.

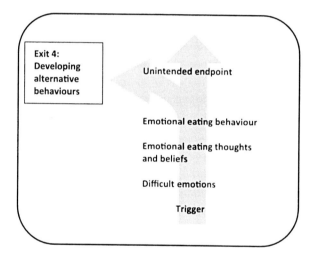

Figure 7.1 Exit 4: Developing alternative behaviours

This is the last of the possible exit routes we are going to focus on in this workbook, and this chapter has been written in collaboration with Dr Esme Banting, Clinical Psychologist. In this chapter, we will focus on some different behavioural options that act as alternatives to emotional eating. We will start by focusing on strategies that you can use whilst you are experiencing the urge to emotionally eat and then move on to consider how you can put some longer-term "behavioural foundations" in place. These "behavioural foundations" focus on developing the skills and strategies to physically and emotionally care for yourself on a more lasting basis. To put this into a slightly different context, if you had back pain, you might need to take medication to get you through the acute phase but then might be doing some longer-term physiotherapy or exercises to prevent future recurrences of back pain.

Part 1

Short term strategies to look after your mind and body

So far in the workbook, we have focused on strategies to manage triggers, emotions, and emotional eating thought processes to exit the familiar emotional eating route. But it is important to acknowledge that there might be times when doing this isn't possible – it may feel too overwhelming or simply not work the way we

DOI: 10.4324/9781032664354-11

are hoping. For the times we might want a break from "brain" work, it is useful to have other options that will help. The first options that we are going to discuss are alternative behaviours that you can try in the moment when you feel overwhelmed with emotions and have the urge to eat. These include sensory/body experiences, distraction, making an active decision to eat and eating mindfully. In effect, these are your "emergency" behavioural strategies to use. In the second part of the chapter, we will focus on building a longer-term approach which involves considering how you treat and look after yourself (this includes how you look after your body and your mind).

Changing your physical state

When we feel overwhelmed by or stuck in an emotion, we can change our emotional state by changing what we feel in our bodies. Rather than just focusing on the brain and the mind, if we change how we feel in our bodies, this has a subsequent effect on the message that the brain receives. So, for example, if you feel physically very tense and your heart is beating quickly, then learning how to get the body into a physically relaxed state sends the brain a message that you are safe. This is a different approach to managing your thoughts, feelings and behaviour – instead of working from brain to body (top down), the following strategies work in the opposite direction (body to brain). We are going to work through a range of strategies that activate different senses in your body.

Move

Shake it off!

Have you ever noticed that animals often "shake it off" after they have a stressful experience? Humans need to be able to do this too! Our bodies hold onto tension when we feel strong emotions. To release this tension, try doing something physically active like dancing around the room to some loud music, swinging your arms and legs or just shaking any parts of your body that feel tense.

Often, just going outside to get some fresh air or moving to a different place can help to break the downward spiral of thoughts and feelings. It won't change the problem, but it might help you to build in a pause. It can break the feeling of being emotionally overwhelmed by giving you some control (you are choosing what you move and where you move to). It's a simple idea, but moving to a different place means that you may literally change your perspective.

Breathe

Breathing can be an incredibly quick and powerful way of changing the way we feel – and the best thing about it is that it's free and available to us 24 hours a day, 7 days a week.

Simply placing your hand on a part of your body where you feel your breath (such as your chest or your stomach) can be a helpful way to bring awareness to and regulate your breathing.

When you notice a moment of stress or intense emotion and you want to feel grounded, calm and focused, you could try square breathing. It's called square breathing because the pattern of breath follows the pattern of drawing four sides of a square:

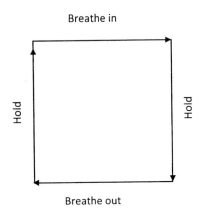

Figure 7.2 Square breathing

For example:

Start by breathing in and counting to four.
Hold your breath for another count of four.
Breathe out for a count of four.
Hold for a count of four.

Repeat for as many cycles as you need.

A slight variation is rectangle breathing. This type of breathing mimics the way we breathe when we are about to fall asleep and sends a signal to our body that it is calm and safe.

In rectangle breathing, we simply make the out breath longer than the in breath.

For example:

Start by breathing in and counting to four.
Hold for a count of four.
Breathe out for a count of six.

Repeat for as many cycles as you need.

Sound

Music is processed by the amygdala (the part of our brain involved in emotions) and is well known for its ability to change our mood.

Feeling stressed out? Create a playlist of sounds that give you an instant sense of relaxation and calm. It doesn't have to be songs with words; it might be ambient music or the sounds of nature (like rain, birds in the forest or waves).

Feeling tired? Music with a tempo of around 150 BPM (beats per minute) can make you feel energised and motivated. Add this to a playlist with songs that remind you of fun and happy times for an extra endorphin boost.

Why not have a go at creating a playlist for the specific emotions that often lead to emotional eating?

Temperature

Our bodies are very responsive to temperature. Holding something warm like a mug of tea or a hot water bottle can help us feel connected, comforted and soothed, particularly in stressful situations, and having a warm bath is a great way to relax and unwind. By contrast, colder temperatures (like splashing ice water on your face or having a cold shower) have the ability to stimulate our vagus nerve and get us out of an energy lull. Give it a try - see what you notice!

Smell

Having familiar, comforting scents can instantly transport us to a place we feel safe and ground us in the present moment. What scents take you to a place of calm? Try lighting a candle or putting a dab of a favourite scent on a tissue or handkerchief to carry with you.

Distraction techniques . . . with a twist

It can be useful to think about what other activities you can do as an alternative to emotional eating. It is useful to do the brain work beforehand so that you have a list of other things that you can do when you feel the urge to emotionally eat. This will help you plan.

You may realise that this approach of using distraction and/or replacing one behaviour with another slightly contradicts the previous emphasis on tuning into what you are feeling and thinking, but ultimately, we have to be pragmatic, and I want you to have a range of skills for different scenarios. I want you to develop flexibility so that you are able to make choices about which strategy will be most helpful in a specific situation - so, for example, there will be times when you are able to really focus on decoding and making space for emotions and updating your beliefs about emotional eating, but there will be other occasions when you simply need to distract yourself.

Build up a list of a few different activities. You might want different ones for different places. These might include things like making a music playlist, going online, having a lie-down, calling or texting a friend, looking at photos, listening to music, painting your nails or applying hand cream/body cream, reading, doing a puzzle, playing a game on your phone, writing an email or letter, organising a drawer or wardrobe, doing a craft, taking a walk etc.

Next time you feel the urge to emotionally eat and you want to respond differently, you could make a commitment to trying three of these activities first. If the three activities haven't worked, you can then make a conscious, active decision about whether you still want to eat. You might also notice that this form of distraction is a sneaky way of getting you to build in a pause (Chapter 4) before eating!

Make active decisions about eating

It would be naïve to simply exclude eating from the range of strategies to manage emotions; it is inevitable that this will happen sometimes. This is the case for most people! It becomes problematic when emotional eating is our default and automatic pattern. If there are still times when you emotionally eat, you could consider introducing some small changes to make it a different eating experience.

Firstly, we want the eating to be less of an automatic process and this involves making some practical changes. Imagine if you were brushing your teeth with the opposite hand that you usually use. It would feel different, and you would feel more conscious of the behaviour. That's exactly the same process we are trying to replicate through making changes to how you eat and the choices you make. Doing this will raise your awareness and shift your attention onto the eating experience. So when you feel the urge to emotionally eat, here are some things to consider and experiment with.

Make the decision to eat an active, informed choice.

Make the choice to eat a conscious (not impulsive) decision. This means exploring your decision to eat – what is driving the decision? How will you feel afterwards? On balance, is it a decision that you are comfortable with? This process involves making an informed, well-considered decision. Please note that this doesn't mean that you "should" decide not to eat – that isn't the aim. The aim is to think through the decision and then come to a point at which you feel at peace with the decision you have made.

Change the eating process

Eat in a different place to usual (different room, chair etc.). This simple step "jolts" the brain out of its automatic shortcuts and will help you pay more attention to your decisions and actions. Storing any tempting foods in a different place (e.g. different cupboard, different container) can make it a less automatic process.

Mindful eating

This is about slowing down but also making sure that you get the most out of the eating experience.

- Put your food on a plate.
- Make eating an experience and pay full attention to the food – zoom in and notice the smell, taste, texture, temperature of the food you have chosen to eat.
- Eat slowly.

Make an active choice about what you will eat and the limits

For example, if you are going to have biscuits, decide how many and put them on a plate (rather than eating from the packet). Often, people have spent a lot of time focusing on trying to completely avoid certain foods (this often rebounds and has the opposite effect), but I think it is more important to build and develop confidence in your ability to manage limited amounts of those foods. It's the "stopping", not the "starting", which is very important.

Reduce secrecy around eating

The secrecy around eating can exacerbate the problem as people get caught up in "spotting the opportunity" when they can eat. It also contributes to feelings of shame and embarrassment. I realise this can be challenging but try to reduce the secrecy around eating. This might involve changing where you eat (e.g. car or bedroom). Over time, you may want to consider talking to anyone you live with about the changes you are making and that from time to time, they will see you eating certain foods in front of them. You might also want to consider how you want them to respond in that situation so you can let them know what you would find helpful (and unhelpful).

Prepare an emotional eating box

Some people find it helpful to plan for emotional eating episodes and prepare an "emotional eating box" for those occasions. The process of planning ahead allows you to consider the type of food and the amount of food that you are going to keep in there.

Part 2

Longer-term strategies to support your behaviour – looking after yourself

In this second half of this chapter, we will focus on developing some longer-term strategies to support your behaviour. This involves considering how you care for and look after yourself. This is important because it determines how we feel and whether our needs are met.

What sort of relationship do you have with yourself?

We don't really spend time thinking about how we speak or behave towards ourselves. We naturally seem to focus on our external relationships with other people rather than our internal relationship with ourselves. The relationship we have with ourselves is the most significant relationship in our lives but the one we often pay least attention to! If you were to describe your relationship with yourself, how would you describe it? Here are some examples of words that might apply: loving, dismissive, critical, caring, challenging, neglectful, negative, supportive.

It is very common for people to prioritise others, but this means that we tend to tune out and neglect our own needs. This, in turn, can then affect our capacity to manage our emotions and the help and support we receive, which can then drive emotional eating as a coping mechanism. The pattern of prioritising other people's needs is often shaped by our early experiences – for example, we may have been brought up to believe that other people's needs have priority over our own or even that attending to other people is a way of getting validation or a way of reducing anxiety. However, if we frequently put our own needs in a lower position to those of others, it sends the brain a message that we are not important and that our needs don't matter.

How does this link to emotional eating? In my clinical experience of working with people with emotional eating patterns, I have found it to be extremely common for people to treat themselves unkindly and unfairly in comparison to the way they treat others. If we learn to pay attention to ourselves and treat ourselves with compassion and understanding, then we are in a better position to manage our emotions and figure out what we need. We are also less likely to rely on food as a way of coping.

Let's just spend a moment thinking about the different ways in which we show or demonstrate our care for others – through the attention we give them, the way we communicate with them and the things we may do for them as well as the way we nurture their well-being. It can be useful to flip this around and think about ways in which we might do the same for ourselves. Whilst comparisons with others can be problematic in many circumstances, in this situation, it can provide us with some useful information about how similarly or differently we treat ourselves and the impact of doing this.

In this next section, we will focus on the following different ways that we take care of and relate to ourselves (and others), including how we pay attention, the things we do, our internal self-talk and the way we care for our body.

How do you pay attention to yourself?

You can think of your attention as being a bit like a spotlight that you shine – you can direct it either externally or internally. Most people are used to focusing the spotlight of their attention externally on other people, but this often means that they don't notice how they are feeling, identify their needs, and look after themselves. If you are tuned out of yourself, how can you figure out what you are feeling or what you might need?

Here are some of the ways in which we might pay attention to others. It is not an exhaustive list, so feel free to add any other examples you can identify.

- Holding other people in mind . . . noticing what they might need or want.
- Noticing if there is a change in them (emotionally, physically etc.).
- Remembering something important about them/their life.
- Providing something they might want, like or need.
- Noticing if they are not present.
- Any others you can identify?

These examples provide an insight into the type of information that you may naturally be gathering about another person's emotional and physical well-being. By paying attention and noticing what is going on for someone, you might find that you are able to provide support or what they may need. So you may find that applying the same principle of paying attention to yourself could work in the same way!

> Reflections on your attention – When you look at the list of examples and consider your own situation, what are the key differences in terms of how much attention you pay to yourself versus others? Are you treating yourself fairly? What are the consequences for you?

One of the fears that people verbalise about paying more attention to themselves is a concern that it might make them a selfish or self-absorbed person. I can assure you that there is a huge difference between being selfish and treating yourself fairly by noticing and addressing your needs! To put this into context, if someone you knew was a parent with two children and they were treating one of the children completely differently to the other, it is highly likely that you would feel very concerned and upset about this. However, this is exactly what many people do to themselves – they treat themselves completely differently to their peers. It might feel uncomfortable at first to start paying more attention to yourself, but it is a new habit, and you need time to practice and adjust. Obviously, you don't have to stop paying attention to others completely (you can still be a supportive friend, parent, partner, colleague etc.), but we are just trying to strike a balance. For now, the aim is to start directing your spotlight of attention internally so you can notice how you are feeling, and what you might need or want.

What do you do for yourself?

There can be a similar process of devoting more time and resources to doing things for others compared to things for yourself. There can be different reasons for this – some practical (e.g. time, busy life, children or adults who are dependent on you) or psychological (e.g. a wish to keep the peace with someone, seeking approval, avoidance of having to focus internally, deflecting attention from the self). This involves shifting from being driven by the need to be liked or to have a quiet life (or whatever other reason there is) to being fair to yourself.

The list that follows contains examples to help you to identify differences in the way you treat yourself versus how you treat others.

- Enquiring about how the other person is feeling.
- Making time/spending time with them.
- Supporting and prioritising their needs/activities.
- Supporting their life to run smoothly.
- Being available to support them if they are distressed or need help.
- Helping them to problem-solve situations.

> Reflections on your behaviour – When you look at the list and consider your own situation, what are the key differences in terms of how and what you do for yourself in comparison to others? Are you treating yourself fairly? What are the consequences for you?

The skill of assertiveness often comes into play when we are thinking about the tendency to prioritise other people's needs over our own. This can be a new skill to learn. Learning to be assertive may mean setting healthy boundaries with others, with work and with yourself so that you can meet your needs in a healthy way. Assertiveness involves valuing yourself and your needs and communicating this. It involves being fair to ourselves and expressing this through our behaviour, in effect saying that our needs are just as important as those of others. This can sometimes create changes in relationship dynamics because other people around you may need to adjust. Hopefully, you will find that the people who really care about you are pleased that you are taking this step.

How do you talk to yourself?

We are now going to focus on how you speak to yourself in comparison to how you speak to others. Usually, when we ask ourselves the classic question of "Would you speak to a friend in the same way that you speak to yourself?" The answer is pretty universally "no"!

HOW DOES YOUR INTERNAL VOICE SOUND?

Try to tune in to your internal voice (we all have one). It is helpful to notice the tone and quality of your internal voice when you speak to yourself compared to when you speak to others. When working with people who are self-critical, I notice that their internal voice often sounds very harsh, judgemental, undermining and bullying. Even if the content of what you say remains the same, just changing the tone can make it sound and feel different – for example, just experiment with saying "Why did I do that?" in a harsh, critical tone compared to a compassionate tone. What are the consequences of using these different tones? What effect does it have?

WHAT DO YOU SAY ABOUT YOURSELF?

In addition to *how* you talk to yourself, *what* you say is also very important. This includes the words, judgements, feedback and the rules and standards you use. The language and content of what people say to themselves is often much harsher and stricter than what they say to others. If we spoke to our friends in the same way we spoke to ourselves, I predict we would have far fewer friends! There is also evidence that when people are self-critical, it tends to be associated with emotional eating behaviour (Varela et al., 2019). This is because self-criticism affects mood, which can then affect eating . . . which then leads to further self-criticism, and the cycle continues.

Sometimes, people have the belief that if they speak harshly to themselves, it will somehow jolt them and motivate them to spring into action (a bit like a stereotypical sergeant major approach of shouting and bullying). However, this is very rarely effective, and usually, these self-critical and negative judgements tend to have the opposite effect of paralysing people so that they freeze and don't act. At the same time as reducing self-criticism, it is important to be accountable for our actions, and this means focusing on showing understanding for our plight but also recognising what we can learn for next time.

Look at the list below to consider some of the ways that you might communicate with others:

- Showing interest – enquiring
- Encouraging them to talk about how they are and their life
- Showing concern for others
- Providing encouragement when things are going well
- Providing support and empathy if struggling
- Raising concerns and being honest about difficulties
- Noticing and spotting when they are being self-critical or overly harsh

> Reflections on your self-talk – When you look at the list and consider your own situation, what are the key differences in terms of how you speak to yourself in comparison to others? Are you treating yourself fairly? What are the consequences for you?

How do you look after your physical and mental well-being?

Many people with weight difficulties have a challenging relationship with their body. Often, people have spent long periods of time being critical and negative about their bodies and can end up being disconnected from it. This means that they can be tuned out of the messages that the body is sending about how it is feeling, what it needs and how to take care of it.

Movement

Find a way to move each day. When you are stuck in a bit of a slump, it can be tempting to cosy up under a duvet and stay on the sofa. But moving our bodies is one of the best ways to take care of our health and give us an instant well-being boost. Movement doesn't have to be a full-on workout at the gym! Going for a walk is a great way to get your circulation moving and increase the production of feel-good chemicals (called endorphins) that help us feel happy and relaxed.

For a bonus well-being boost, try exercising in nature. Humans evolved to spend time outside. Whether it's a green space (like a park or wood), a blue space (like rivers or coasts) or an urban space (like trees on a street, local gardens or even watching a nature documentary), finding nature wherever you are can help manage stress, relieve feelings of tiredness and improve energy and concentration. Breathing in fresh air and getting daylight each day can boost vitamin D levels and support our immune system to fight off illness.

On days when your body is telling you it needs to rest, give yourself permission to try a more gentle form of movement, like stretching. Notice any feelings of tightness or stiffness in your body and move in any way you feel you need.

Soak in moments of joy

We can find joy in the smallest of moments, on even the darkest of days . . . but we do have to actively look for it. The human mind evolved with an inbuilt bias to focus on and remember all the negative things that happen. Once upon a time, this enabled our ancestors to learn from threats and protect them against danger. But now, this means we need to work a lot harder to notice and remember the positive things that happen, because when we live our lives on autopilot, we easily miss them.

Train your brain to soak in moments of joy.

All of these moments add up to give us a sense of well-being. The key is to notice them and then take a moment to soak in their joy. Noticing these moments (as well as the negative ones we are wired to notice) helps us to find a sense of balance in our minds and our lives.

The more we practice looking for moments of joy, the more we will find them, and the better our sense of well-being will be. Whilst you are practicing, it can be helpful to jot these moments down in a journal or even take a photo of them to look back on at the end of each day.

Sleep

Getting enough sleep is one of the most important ways we can take care of our bodies.

The amount of sleep each person needs varies, but the recommended average is around 8 hours per night. To give yourself the best chance of getting a good night's sleep, the following tips can be helpful:

- Get up and go to bed at the same time each day. This helps your body clock get into a routine and know when to get sleepy and when to wake up.
- Get some sunlight first thing in the morning – even if it's just a few short moments. This will help regulate your circadian rhythm and tell your body when to trigger sleepiness later that night.
- Disconnect from screens and other stimulating activities before bed and have a good wind-down routine. Our bodies and minds need time to prepare for sleep. Using soft lighting can help create a calming environment.
- If racing thoughts stop you falling asleep or wake you up in the night, try keeping a notebook by your bed. Write your thoughts down when they come to you so you don't have to worry about remembering them (this can stop you getting back to sleep). You can be reassured that you have noted the thoughts and will deal with them the next day.
- Limit your caffeine and alcohol intake, since both these things can reduce the quality of sleep you get.
- There is support and treatment available for sleep problems. If you are worried about the impact that sleep is having on your well-being, speak to your GP.

Nourish and hydrate

It is hard (if not impossible!) for us to function optimally when our body isn't getting the energy or nutrition it needs to survive.

It is important that we eat regular meals with foods that are satisfying for both body *and* mind.

Make it a priority to eat food regularly throughout the day. Try to include a wide variety of foods that will give you all the nutrients and energy you need *and* that you look forward to and enjoy. Meeting our physical and psychological hunger needs in this way reduces the chances that cravings will build and lead to out-of-control eating taking place. As discussed in Chapter 1, eating regularly provides a safety net that can help to prevent big fluctuations in your mood and appetite.

Set an intention to get enough water each day. Did you know our bodies are made up of 60% water? We need enough fluid to function well and keep our body systems working, but it's easy to stop paying attention to our thirst signals or feel too busy to make time to drink regularly. To avoid becoming dehydrated, it can be useful to set a reminder on your phone or keep track of how much water you are drinking by using a water bottle with measurements on it.

Rest

We live in a world in which being busy is seen as a sign of success, and rest can be hard to come by. Food can become a justification to take a pause in our otherwise busy days and endless to-do lists. But rest is essential to maintain good mental health and productivity. After all, you can't pour from an empty cup!

Give yourself permission to slow down and re-charge your batteries. How often do you let your phone battery die? Usually, this is something we go to great lengths to avoid. But when it comes to our own battery, it's another story entirely!

Plan in moments of rest each day. Sometimes, scheduling time to rest is the only way to ensure it gets the time it needs. Rest can be slow and relaxing (such as sitting quietly, having a bath, reading a book) or active and social (like exercising, engaging in a hobby or spending time with friends). The key is to find a balance between activities that are depleting (drain your battery) and restorative (those that charge it back up again).

Connect

Humans have evolved to be social beings, and feeling connected is vital for our well-being. Sometimes, we become disconnected from the people in our lives and the things that are important to us. Eating can become a way of filling a void when we feel something is missing.

Things to try when you want to feel more connected:

- Reach out to a loved one
- Spend time with a pet
- Spend time in nature
- Journal
- Practice gratitude
- Re-connect with a hobby
- Create something
- Learn something new
- Volunteer

Caring for yourself and creating long-term supportive foundations

In this chapter, we have focused on how you look after yourself. This includes how much attention you give to yourself, what you do for yourself, how you speak to yourself and how you care for your body. The next step is to identify any changes or shifts that you want to make in these different areas. For example:

- Attention: If you were to pay more attention to yourself and your needs, what might you do more of?
- Behaviour: If you were to do more things for yourself, what would you be doing?
- Self-talk: If you were to talk differently to yourself (both tone and content), what type of things might you say?
- Body care: If you wanted to introduce or reconnect with some ways of looking after your body, what would you do?

	What do I want to do more of?	How can I plan to make this happen?
Paying attention - noticing and recognising how you are and what you need/want		
Behaviour – what you do for yourself		
Self-talk - how and what you say to yourself		
Body and well-being - how and what you do to look after your body		

Key points and tasks to work on

- We have made a distinction between short-term behaviours that you can use as a way of diverting yourself from emotional eating and putting in place the longer-term behavioural foundations necessary to look after yourself and your needs.
- It is helpful to identify some "instant" behaviours that you can use as an alternative to emotional eating. These include different sensory exercises (breathing etc.) as well as distraction techniques and mindful eating.
- We also identified ways in which you can develop your self-care by treating yourself fairly with your attention, behaviour, self-talk and the way you care for your body and mind.

Next steps

The next steps are to experiment with testing out some of these changes to see whether this makes a difference to identifying your own needs and how you treat yourself. If you treat yourself with understanding and compassion, you have got more chance of managing your emotional health and meeting your needs without reverting to using food to do so. As mentioned before, you may not always feel comfortable whilst experimenting with these changes. This is a work in progress, so it will take time to get used to creating more space for yourself.

Reference

Varela, C., Andres, A., & Saldana, C. (2019). The behavioral pathway model to overweight and obesity: Coping strategies, eating behaviors and body mass index. *Eating and Weight Disorders Studies on Anorexia, Bulimia and Obesity.* https:// doi.org/10.1007/s40519-019-00760-2

Section 3

Template

Chapter 8
Developing your emotional eating template

In this final section, we are going to bring together all the information, insight and strategies you have gathered in Section 1 and Section 2 to generate your new emotional eating template. We will also identify ways in which you can respond to and manage the inevitable setbacks that will occur as you develop new skills.

In the first part of the book, we focused on developing an understanding of:

1 how the emotional eating route was created
2 what the emotional eating route currently looks like

We reviewed the different landmarks along the way that lead to emotional eating and the consequences associated with it (the unintended endpoint of the route). Here is a list of the different topics and areas that we identified as part of the emotional eating route . . . it just goes to show how much is involved in the process of emotional eating!

Emotional eating route	Which landmarks have you identified?
Early experiences related to eating and weight	
Early/important messages about emotions	
Associations and beliefs that formed about food/mood based on early experiences	
Triggers for emotional eating	
Your reactions to triggers and interpretation of triggers (thinking patterns and self-talk)	
Specific emotions connected with emotional eating	
Thought processes associated with emotional eating – "want" thoughts, "decision" thoughts and underlying emotional eating beliefs (the original "good reason")	
Characteristics of the emotional eating behaviour	
Your intended destination – your short-term rationale for emotional eating (i.e. how it might help with your emotions in the moment).	
Your unintended endpoint – the longer-term psychological and physical consequences of the emotional eating	
Any others?	

DOI: 10.4324/9781032664354-13

When you review this list, are there any missing areas that you need to go back to? You might also want to refer to the original emotional eating route that you completed at the end of Section 1.

We then started to consider the different options for diverting and re-routing from the original emotional eating route. This involved identifying ways to manage triggers by building in a pause, learning to understand and manage emotions differently, learning to identify and manage your emotional eating thoughts and, finally, identifying different behaviours as a short-term and longer-term alternative to emotional eating.

Here is a list of the strategies that we identified:

Possible exits from your emotional eating route	Which skills are most relevant and important to help you manage your emotional eating?
Building in a pause - slowing the body and mind	
Identifying and questioning your reaction to triggers - building perspective, zooming out	
Understanding emotions - challenging myths and updating our understanding of emotions	
Identifying the meaning of emotions - decoding the signal	
Managing emotions - making space	
Identifying your emotional eating thought ladder and emotional eating thought patterns	
Learning to observe thoughts through defusion	
Learning to challenge decision-based thoughts	
Updating underlying emotional eating beliefs	
Finding alternative behaviours - body work/sensory practices	
Distraction techniques	
Making an active decision to eat - mindful eating	
Developing longer-term behavioural foundations to looking after your mind and body	
Any others?	

Creating your alternative Emotional Eating route

You might want to refer to the map of your automatic emotional eating route that you constructed at the end of Section 1. We now want to add some diversions to the route which you will build on through experimenting with the different strategies and skills we have discussed. This is a way of consolidating what you have learned and setting your intentions for the future. It is good to add these to your emotional eating route because this creates your new template or route for the future, and you can see where the strategies might divert the flow of your automatic route. You can use this as a reference point in future and add, build and amend it as needed. It is helpful to keep the template of your new emotional eating route under review to reflect on how it is working and where tweaks may be needed.

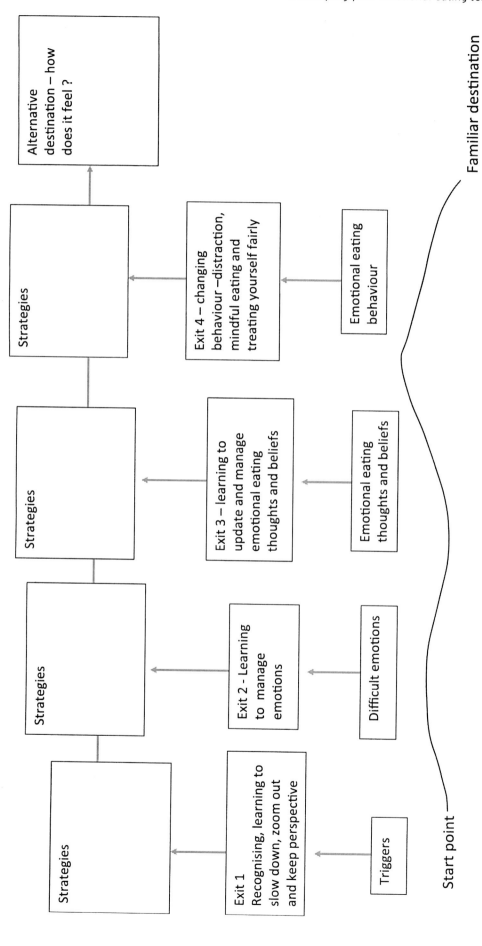

Figure 8.1 Emotional eating route with exits and strategies

Noticing what happens when you take a different route – what is the outcome?

Now that you are starting to experiment with using different skills and strategies to help you re-route from emotional eating, it is also worth noticing your new endpoint for this route.

When you try this new approach and make a different choice, e.g. to manage your emotions or to manage your reactions to triggers, then how do you feel afterwards?

- What do you notice?

- How do you feel about yourself (in comparison with when you emotionally eat)?

- What are the benefits of this?

- Are there any costs?

- What are the next steps?

It is important to take note of the positive steps you are taking and what is going well for you. We naturally tend to focus on what we are not doing or the times when things haven't gone according to plan, and this often leads to a skewed perception of our overall progress. I hope that you will give yourself credit for having the courage to learn something different and to try new things.

Managing setbacks – when you revert to the original route

Although mapping out your new emotional eating route is a helpful, proactive step that might help you navigate around hazards, it is inevitable that it won't always go to plan, and there will be setbacks along the way. It is a reality that you are likely to continue to experience triggers, difficult emotions and challenging thoughts – this is normal and a natural part of being human. Your mind will want to continue automatically following the familiar, well-established emotional eating route, so it is inevitable and normal that you will flip between the old route and the new route at times. It is therefore important that we factor setbacks in and plan how you can respond to them. Based on my experience, I would be more puzzled and confused if a setback didn't happen! It is what you do after the setback that really matters, not the setback itself.

Often, people slip into being self-critical after an emotional eating setback – they often berate, belittle and condemn themselves. This inevitably has a negative impact on mood. If you step back and think about the way you speak to yourself after you have had a setback, would you realistically imagine that you would speak to someone else like that? Would you use those words and express yourself with that tone of voice? What would you say? What tone of voice would you use? What would your facial expression show?

There is also a pattern of people resetting strict "diet" intentions after a setback whereby they become overly restrictive with their eating, and inevitably this is not sustainable. Some research (Varela et al., 2019) found that self-critical thinking was associated with both emotional eating and restrictive eating, and this is because people often try to double down and set tough, harsh dieting rules after an emotional eating episode. However, this just tends to create further issues and perpetuates the cycle (as well as making people unhappy).

Dealing with self-critical thoughts after a setback

There is lots of evidence that self-critical thinking tends to block people's attempts to make changes and that a compassionate approach is a much more helpful approach.

Just stop for a second and identify someone who you think of as being a bully – it might be someone that you know personally or someone who is well known (maybe a politician or someone from the sports or entertainment world). Imagine that this bully observed someone making a mistake or not doing something 100% correctly. How would the bully react? It is highly likely that they would draw attention to the mistake, they would emphasise the mistake and make it seem like a big deal, they might humiliate or use judgemental language and so on. Bullies try to assume power to make the other person feel submissive. You might wonder why I am spending time talking about bullying, but if you look at the actions of the bully, you might recognise that there is some similarity with how you treat or speak to yourself after having an emotional eating setback. Often, people tend to make nasty comments about themselves ("I'm such a failure. I've got no willpower"), they lose perspective ("I've ruined everything. I'll never be able to do it") and experience feelings of shame (submissive). The psychologist Paul Gilbert suggested that people who are highly self-critical have an "internal bully" or inner critic (2009).

I now want you to imagine what you would do if you were going to step in to support someone who was being bullied. I imagine that you might encourage them to focus on the things they have achieved, encourage them to keep things in perspective, turn their attention away from the bully, praise them for their commitment whilst encouraging future learning etc. Can you imagine the difference in how the person might feel?

Is compassion a way of "letting yourself off the hook"?

Learning to be compassionate is not about "letting yourself off the hook" - it is about holding yourself accountable whilst also acknowledging that you are trying your best and learning from your experiences. It is a way of acknowledging that you are learning new skills, and this takes time and practice. Nobody would expect that you would be fully competent at driving a car after your first lesson! Learning involves encountering setbacks and making mistakes.

It is also worth remembering all the steps that were involved in learning the automatic emotional eating route in the first place. That didn't happen quickly or in response to a single situation; it took repetition over a long period of time for the pattern to develop (that's how and why it became automatic!). Also, as you can see from the emotional eating map that you created, there are many steps and processes involved in creating and following the emotional eating route (these were probably out of awareness before). It therefore makes sense that it will take some time to learn new skills and to develop a new pathway and route in your brain. I hope that you will be able to acknowledge that this is a challenging process whilst giving yourself credit for engaging with it.

Who is your compassionate supporter?

Sometimes, it can be hard to find your own compassionate voice at first. People have often experienced many years of hearing and listening to the bullying, critical voice. You might want to think about people around you who are compassionate so you can try to imagine how they might respond and what they may say. They may be people you know . . . friends, family, colleagues etc. However, sometimes it is a sad reality that people don't always have many compassionate voices around them, so in this situation, it can be useful to think about well-known figures that you admire (e.g. in the public eye or figures from history/media/politics) or even pets. Try to imagine what words they might use or how they might show and demonstrate compassion (they may softly touch your hand or rub your shoulder). Even imagining these experiences helps to create new pathways in the brain. How do you feel when you receive a compassionate response? What happens in your mind and your body? How does it help you engage with continuing your efforts to make changes to your emotional eating?

How does the way you speak to yourself after a setback impact the next steps you take?

I now want you to imagine the effect of these two different approaches (self-critical versus compassionate) on a person's behaviour.

Bullying/blaming style	Compassionate style - helpful, balanced, supportive thoughts
Thoughts You're useless. What on earth made you think you could ever do this? You've got zero willpower. You are never going to change things. ↓ **Impact on behaviour** Person is paralysed by fear and shame, so they "freeze" and do nothing. OR Person chooses a radical option (i.e. plans to drastically restrict calories) but one which is not sustainable so will trigger another setback.	**Thoughts** OK, things didn't go as well as I hoped they would, but I am trying to learn a different approach, and it is not realistic to think it will go smoothly all the time. What can I take from this experience to help next time? What can I do differently? ↓ **Impact on behaviour** Person views it as a learning process and continues to engage - they hold themselves accountable for the setback but build on their experiences. Gets back on track with new knowledge to adjust plan.

In the table that follows, write down some of the things you might typically say to yourself after a setback. Now, try to step back and write down a compassionate, helpful response instead. If you find it difficult to do this then you might find it easier to imagine what you might say to support a friend in a similar situation.

Usual thoughts after a setback	Helpful, balanced, supportive thoughts
_____ _____ _____ _____ _____ ↓ **What impact do these thoughts have on your behaviour? What do you do in response?** _____ _____ _____	_____ _____ _____ _____ _____ ↓ **What impact do these thoughts have on your behaviour? What do you do in response?** _____ _____ _____

Managing your behaviour after a setback

Remember that when you catch yourself on the automatic emotional eating route, there is always a new decision point coming up. You can make a choice at any stage; it is not a foregone conclusion that you continue along the emotional eating route. Setbacks are not permanent because you can always reroute. Think about what steps or choices you can make to exit the route or find an alternative option. It doesn't have to be anything radical; small changes can make a difference to how you feel.

The start of your solo journey . . .

I hope that this workbook has provided you with some new tools to understand and to create some alternatives to your old emotional eating route. I hope you feel better equipped with some new navigational and re-routing skills. I wish you strength, courage, hope and compassion on your new route. Thank you for allowing me to accompany you to this point. I wish you well on the rest of your journey.

References

Gilbert, P. (2009). *Overcoming depression: A self-help guide using cognitive behavioural techniques.* Robinson.

Varela, C., Andres, A., & Saldana, C. (2019). The behavioral pathway model to overweight and obesity: Coping strategies, eating behaviors and body mass index. *Eating and Weight Disorders - Studies on Anorexia, Bulimia and Obesity.* https://doi.org/10.1007/s40519-019-00760-2

Index

Note: Page numbers in *italics* indicate a figure on the corresponding page.